Systematic Reviews

Carole Torgerson

Continuum International Publishing Group
The Tower Building
11 York Road
London SE1 7NX

15 East 26th Street
New York
NY 10010

British Library Cataloguing-in-Publication Data
A catalogue record for this book is available from the British Library.

ISBN 0 8264 6580 3 (paperback)

Library of Congress Cataloging-in-Publication Data
A catalog record for this book is available from the Library of Congress.

Typeset by BookEns Ltd, Royston, Herts.
Printed and bound in Great Britain by MPG Books Ltd, Bodmin, Cornwall

Contents

Series Editor's Introduction

The Continuum Research Methods series aims to provide undergraduate, Masters and research students with accessible and authoritative guides to particular aspects of research methodology. Each title looks specifically at one topic and gives it in-depth treatment, very much in the tradition of the Rediguide series of the 1960s and 1970s.

Such an approach allows students to choose the books that are most appropriate to their own projects, whether they are working on a short dissertation, a medium-length work (15–40 000 words) or a fully-fledged thesis at MPhil or PhD level. Each title includes examples of students' work, clear explication of the principles and practices involved, and summaries of how best to check that your research is on course.

In due course, individual titles will be combined into larger books and, subsequently, into encyclopaedic works for reference.

The series will also be of use to researchers designing funded projects, and to supervisors who wish to recommend in-depth help to their research students.

Richard Andrews

Acknowledgements

Tables 4.3, 4.4 and 5.3, and figure 6.2 were previously published in Torgerson *et al.* (2003), 'A systematic review and meta-analysis of randomised controlled trials evaluating interventions in adult literacy and numeracy', *Journal of Research in Reading*, 26(3), (tables 1, 2 and 5, and figure 1) (copyright-holder UK Reading Association).

Tables 7.1 and 7.2 and figure 7.1 were previously published in Torgerson *et al.* (2002), 'Do volunteers in schools help children learn to read? A systematic review of randomised controlled trials', *Educational Studies*, 28(4), 433–44 (tables I and II and figure 1) (see http://www.tandf.-co.uk).

Tables 4.3, 4.4, and 5.3, box 4.3 and figures 6.1 and 6.2 were previously produced in a report to the National Research and Development Centre for Adult Literacy and Numeracy (Torgerson, Brooks *et al.* 2003, *Adult literacy and numeracy interventions and outcomes: expert, scoping and systematic reviews of the trial literature*) (tables 4.1 and 4.2. from 'scoping' review; tables 3.2 and figures 3.1 and 3.2 from 'systematic review of RCTs'; first table in Appendix E).

I acknowledge the influence of the methods of NHS CRO and the EPPI Centre on some of the ideas in the book.

I thank Richard Andrews (University of York) and Greg Brooks (University of Sheffield) for their helpful comments on an earlier version of the manuscript.

I thank David Torgerson (University of York) for suggesting examples and comparisons from health care policy and research, and Alison Robinson (University of York) for proof reading the manuscript.

Scope of the Book

The focus of this book is on systematic reviews and meta-analyses of randomized controlled trials in educational research. Systematic reviews can be used to synthesize studies of other designs, such as longitudinal studies, non-randomized controlled trials or qualitative research (Gough and Elbourne 2002). However, the randomized controlled trial (RCT) is widely acknowledged to be the 'gold standard' of effectiveness research, and systematic reviews of RCTs the gold standard in effectiveness research synthesis. In effectiveness research in education, the randomized controlled trial is the most robust method of establishing 'what works'. Systematic reviews can facilitate the definition of a future research agenda, and inform the evidence-base for policy-making and effective professional practice. This book is aimed at students and researchers who wish to undertake a systematic review for the first time. It includes a step-by-step description of the rationale for and the processes involved in undertaking systematic reviews and meta-analyses.

Glossary

Attrition – Often participants are lost during a trial and cannot be included in the analysis. This is termed attrition or is sometimes known as mortality.

Bias – A term denoting that a known or unknown variable (rather than the intervention) is, or may be, responsible for an observed effect.

Concealed allocation – This is where the researchers, participants and teachers are prevented from knowing in advance the allocation of an individual. Random allocation can be undermined by selection of participants to be in a desired group. Fair randomization will, on average, produce equivalent groups. Using 'open' randomization methods such as random number tables means that the researcher will know the next allocation in advance of it happening. Therefore, in theory the next participant could be 'excluded' from the study if he/she does not possess certain 'desirable' characteristics. This can then lead to bias, which undermines the whole basis of random allocation. It is important, therefore, that the 'mechanics' of randomization are clearly described to assess whether or not the study is susceptible to 'subversion' bias.

Confidence intervals – The point estimate of effect of any intervention will always be imprecise. The level of the imprecision is dependent upon the sample size and event rate in the treatment groups. The use of confidence intervals (usually 95%, but sometimes 99% or 90%) reflects this imprecision in the study results. Thus, for example, a treatment that has an effect size of 0.50, but a confidence interval of –0.1 to 1.2 is not statistically significant but will indicate to the reader that there is a relatively high possibility that there is a beneficial effect of treatment in excess of 1 standard deviation. In this instance, one might consider doing a further, larger randomized trial. In contrast, if the point effect is 0.05 and the confidence interval is −0.1 to 0.12 then the reader might consider that it is unlikely even with a bigger trial that this intervention would show an educationally significant effect (assuming the conduct of the trial in question is of high quality).

CONSORT – Consolidated Standards for Reporting Trials is the methodological standard adopted by many medical journals for publication of randomized controlled trials.

Controlled trial (CT) – This usually means a study with a control group that has been formed by means other than randomization. Consequently the validity of the study using this design is potentially threatened by selection bias.

Co-variates or confounders – These are variables that are associated with outcome. Randomization is the only method that ensures that both known and unknown co-variates are equally distributed among treatment groups.

Effect size – When an outcome variable is measured on a continuous scale (e.g. changes in a test score) the improvement or decrement is described in standard deviation units, which is termed the effect size.

Funnel plot – A method of assessing whether there is any publication bias. The effect size of each study is plotted against its sample size. Small studies will have large random variations in their effect sizes, which will be scattered along the x-axis close to the bottom of the y-axis. Larger studies will be higher up on the y-axis and less scattered along the x-axis. A review with no publication bias will show a plot in the shape of an inverted funnel.

ITT analysis – Intention to Teach – This is where all participants are analysed in their original randomized groups; it is the most robust analytical method. Once participants have been allocated to their respective groups it is important that they remain in those groups for analysis, to avoid bias. A common, but incorrect, method is to exclude some participants after randomization for a variety of reasons. One approach is to do what is termed 'an on-treatment analysis' – this is where only those participants who demonstrate treatment fidelity are included in the analysis. Unfortunately, this can lead to bias, as those participants who complete treatment are likely to be different from those who do not. Intervention-received analysis can therefore produce a biased result.

Paired randomization – This is a commonly used method in educational research. Participants are formed into matched pairs on the basis of important co-variates (e.g. gender and/or pre-test scores). Once the study group has been formed into pairs a random member of each pair is allocated to the intervention. The consequence of pairing is that there should be exactly equal numbers in each group and the group should be exactly balanced in terms of the characteristics on which the pairing took place. If the co-variate used for pairing (e.g. age) has an unusual relationship with outcome this cannot be explored in the analysis as the pairing eliminates all variation due to that co-variate.

Publication bias – Not all RCTs are published. There is a well-established tendency for trials that produce negative effects or null effects to be less likely to be published than positive trials. Unless a systematic review includes these negative trials it can give a misleading optimistic assessment of the intervention. Existence of publication bias can be detected by using funnel plots.

Randomized Controlled Trial (RCT) – This is where two or more groups have been formed through random allocation (or a similar method). This is the only method that ensures that selection bias is eliminated at baseline.

Regression to the mean – This statistical phenomenon occurs when test results are, by chance, some distance away from the mean. Consequently at post-testing the 'extreme' results will tend to regress to the mean. When selecting participants on extreme test results (e.g. very poor pre-tests) there will be an apparent dramatic improvement on post-test because of this effect (irrespective of the teaching method). Randomization automatically controls for regression to the mean effects. Nevertheless, it can still have an influence if the groups are unbalanced at baseline on pre-test scores. This imbalance can be adjusted for by a multivariate analysis.

Sample size calculations – Trials in educational research commonly exhibit a Type II error. This is where the sample size is insufficient to show, as statistically significant, a difference that is educationally important. Reviews of educational interventions have shown that most interventions will, at best, only lead to an improvement in the region of half a standard deviation and quite often somewhat less. Statistical theory shows that to reliably detect (with 80% power) half a standard deviation difference as statistically significant ($p = 0.05$) for a normally distributed variable requires a minimum sample size of 126 participants. Studies that are smaller than this risk erroneously concluding that there was not a significant difference when actually there was. Therefore, a good-quality study ought to describe the reasoning behind the choice of sample size.

Selection bias – This occurs when groups are formed by a process other than randomization and means that important factors that are associated with outcome differ between the groups *before* they are exposed to the intervention.

Standard deviation – A measure of spread or dispersion of continuous data. A high standard deviation implies that the values are widely scattered relative to the mean value, while a small value implies the converse.

1

Background: Evidence-based Education

Evidence-based policy-making

Since the late 1990s an increasingly high profile of 'evidence-based' policy-making in education and the social sciences has emerged in the UK (Davies 1999, Davies 2000, Constable and Coe 2000, Davies, Laycock *et al.* 2000, Evans and Benefield 2001, Young *et al.* 2002, Gough and Elbourne 2002). The movement towards evidence-based education clearly derives, in part, from similar, earlier developments in health care research. In the early 1990s health care research became dominated by the need to inform policy-making through the use of rigorous evidence from research synthesis. For example, the Cochrane Collaboration was established in Oxford in 1993 (http://www.cochrane.org). Its remit was to undertake systematic reviews of health care interventions through the work of 50 'review groups' in various fields of health care. The National Health Service Centre for Reviews and Dissemination at the University of York (NHS CRD) (http://www.york.ac.uk/inst/crd/srinfo/htm) was established at around the same time to undertake systematic reviews in health care policy. A key element in the recent development of evidence-based education is a renewed focus on systematic review methodology and methods in this field.

A number of reasons have been suggested for the rise of

evidence-based policy, including developments in information technology in general and in electronic databases in particular (Davies, Nutley, Smith 2000). The impetus towards evidence-based education occurred at around the same time as the debate about the value and methods of educational research in the late 1990s (see for example, Hargreaves 1996, Hargreaves 1997, Hammersley 1997, Tooley and Darby 1998). Various criticisms were levelled at the educational research community, most notably for its lack of scientific rigour, quality and relevance. A detailed analysis of the debate is beyond the scope of this book. It has been well documented elsewhere (Sebba in Davies, Laycock *et al.* 2000, Davies 2000, Pring 2000, Evans and Benefield 2001, Pirrie 2001, Oakley 2002). However, links between the debate and the rise of the evidence-based education movement have been suggested (Pirrie 2001, Oakley 2002). The trend towards 'evidence-based' and then 'evidence-informed' policy extended to spheres in the social sciences, including health promotion in the early 1990s, and education in the late 1990s and into the beginning of the twenty-first century. Recent significant national and international developments in evidence-based educational and social research have raised the profile of the movement.

In 1997 a series of biennial conferences entitled 'Evidence-based Policies and Indicator Systems' (http://cem.dur.ac.uk/ebeuk) was established at the University of Durham. At the time of the first conference in 1997 the concept of 'evidence-based' policy outside the field of health care was still fairly 'marginal' (Constable and Coe 2000).

Recently, two evidence-based initiatives have been established in the UK to play prominent roles in the 'evidence-based policy' (EBP) debate. The Centre for Evidence-Based Policy and Practice was established in December 2000 (funded by the Economic and Social Research Council) at Queen Mary, University of London (http://www.evidencenetwork.org), to 'advance' the debate about evidence-based policy and practice (see Young *et al.* 2002).

The Evidence for Policy and Practice Information and Co-ordinating Centre (EPPI-Centre) (http://www.ioe.ac.uk/projects.html) within the Social Science Research Unit at the Institute of Education, University of London, began undertaking systematic reviews in health promotion (funded by the Department of Health) in 1993. In 2000 the Department for Education and Skills (DfES) funded the Centre to support a series of systematic reviews in educational research (http://eppi.ioe.ac.uk/EPPIWeb/home.aspx), to inform policy, practice and 'democratic debate' (Gough and Elbourne 2002). This initiative is based on the Cochrane Collaboration model: a number of collaborative review groups have been set up to undertake systematic reviews in various areas of educational research. (For detailed analyses of the work of the EPPI-Centre see Sebba in Davies, Laycock *et al.* 2000, Evans and Benefield 2001, Gough and Elbourne 2002, Oakley 2002.) Another UK initiative occurred in 2003: the Teacher Training Agency commissioned a series of systematic reviews, relevant to initial teacher training and supported by the EPPI-Centre.

Another important recent development in social and educational research has been the establishing of the Campbell Collaboration Social, Psychological, Educational and Criminological Trials Register (C2-SPECTR) in February 2000 in the USA. Its aims are to identify all the experimental research of educational, social policy and criminal justice interventions (http://campbell.gse.upenn.edu/), and to undertake, update and make accessible systematic reviews of social and educational interventions (Petrosino *et al.* 2000). The Campbell Collaboration mirrors the earlier Cochrane Collaboration. Indeed, the C2-SPECTR initiative arose directly out of the work of the Cochrane Developmental, Psychosocial and Learning

Problems Group, and was influenced by the methodology and methods developed in the Cochrane Collaboration (Petrosino *et al.* 2000).

The need for reviews

These initiatives and others developed from the realization that a single experiment seeking to investigate the effectiveness of an educational policy, no matter how well conducted, is limited by 'time-, sample- and context-specificity' (Davies 2000). A single study should not be considered in isolation, but positioned within the 'totality' of research in a field to give a more complete picture (Mulrow 1994, Chalmers *et al.* 2002).

Government policy in the UK has not always taken cognizance of systematic reviews, sometimes preferring the results of single studies. In 2000 the government introduced a 'driver education' programme on the basis of positive results from a single study (Clayton *et al.* 1998). Yet a systematic review of trials found that the introduction of driver education into schools actually led to an *increase* in injuries and road traffic accidents among younger drivers (Cochrane Injuries Group Driver Education Review 2001). This counter-intuitive finding was explained by the fact that young people who had participated in the driver education programmes tended to start to learn to drive earlier compared with young people who had attended control schools and therefore not participated in the programme.

There are other problems with single studies. The results of an educational experiment undertaken in the USA might not be generalizable to the UK educational context. However, if a series of high-quality experiments have been undertaken recently in the USA, Canada, Australia and New Zealand and if they are sufficiently similar in terms of sample and context, and are found to yield similar results in a systematic research synthesis, one might, in the absence of any UK evidence, be confident that the effects could transfer to a UK setting.

Traditional narrative literature review

The traditional literature review often forms the basis of 'opinion' pieces, 'expert' reviews or students' theses, but is less helpful for guiding policy or contributing to an informed debate of the issues. This is due to a number of factors. The research literature included in traditional narrative reviews tends to be a 'biased' sample of the full range of the literature on the subject. It is usually undertaken through the perspective of the reviewer who gathers and interprets the literature in a given field. The reasons for including some studies and excluding others are often not made explicit, and may reflect the biases of the author. Included references may be used to support the 'expert opinion' whilst other references that contradict this opinion may be excluded from the review. If the search strategy and inclusion criteria have not been made explicit it will not be possible for the review to be replicated by a third party. Because a 'systematic, rigorous and exhaustive' search of all the relevant literature (Davies 2000) has not been undertaken, relevant studies could have been excluded from the review, leading to potential selection and/or publication bias. Failure to include all the appropriate studies may lead to incorrect interpretations of the evidence. Finally, usually in traditional literature reviews the individual studies are not quality assessed before inclusion in the review, and therefore there may be no differentiation between methodologically 'sound' and 'unsound' studies (Young *et al.* 2002). The shortcomings of the 'expert' review are well recognized in evidence-based health care, where in the hierarchy of evidence 'expert opinion' constitutes the lowest grade of evidence. Nevertheless, they remain influential in all areas of social research.

Systematic review

A more rigorous alternative to the 'narrative' review is the systematic review. A systematic review differs from a traditional narrative review in that its methods are explicit and open to scrutiny. It seeks to identify *all* the available evidence with respect to a given theme. Systematic reviews have the advantage of including all the studies in a field (sometimes positive and negative studies), so the reader can judge using the *totality* of evidence whether the evidence supports or refutes a given hypothesis. This evidence is collected, screened for quality and synthesized into an overall summary of the research in the field. Because all the evidence pertaining to a given topic is included in the systematic review, with rejected evidence catalogued and the reasons for rejection made explicit, the resulting findings are often less susceptible to selection, publication and other biases than those of a traditional or 'non-systematic' review.

Rationale for systematic reviews

The rationale for undertaking a systematic review has been well rehearsed in the fields of health care (for example, Egger *et al.* 2001, Chalmers *et al.* 2002), social and educational research (for example, Evans and Benefield 2001, Oakley 2002). It is a scientifically rigorous method for summarizing the results of primary research and for checking consistency among such studies (Petticrew 2001). The rationale for systematic reviews in medicine is firmly embedded in the 'positivist' or 'scientific' tradition or paradigm (Mulrow 1994). Systematic reviews are traditionally associated with meta-analyses of research based on quantitative epistemological traditions and methodologies (Badger *et al.* 2000, Hammersley 2001). The most important aspect of the scientific paradigm is that a study must be replicable as well as reliable and credible. Judgements and assumptions are made explicit to allow exposure to scrutiny and comment. In education (and health) the methodology is currently being extended to encompass studies using a broad range of methods including qualitative research (Petticrew 2001).

Mulrow (1994), writing about systematic reviews and meta-analyses in the field of health care, has outlined some assumptions on which this rationale is based. Systematic review methodology has the ability to manage potentially 'unmanageable amounts of information', and rationalize existing evidence efficiently by establishing whether research findings are consistent and generalizable, and to explain why if they are not. Often similar studies can be put together, statistically, in a meta-analysis. Meta-analyses can be used to increase power and precision in the measurement of effect sizes. Finally, systematic reviews use scientific methods that reduce 'random and systematic errors of bias' (Mulrow 1994). Clearly such a rationale does not apply exclusively to research in health care.

Aims of a systematic review

The aims of a systematic review are well documented in the health care (Mulrow, 1994, Egger *et al.* 2001, Petticrew 2001, Chalmers *et al.* 2002) and social policy literature (Davies 1999, Davies 2000, Badger *et al.* 2000, Gough and Elbourne 2002, Young *et al.* 2002). They are:

(i) to address a specific (well focused, relevant) question;
(ii) to search for, locate and collate the results of the research in a systematic way;

(iii) to reduce bias at all stages of the review (publication, selection and other forms of bias);
(iv) to appraise the quality of the research in the light of the research question;
(v) to synthesize the results of the review in an explicit way;
(vi) to make the knowledge base more accessible;
(vii) to identify gaps; to place new proposals in the context of existing knowledge;
(viii) to propose a future research agenda; to make recommendations;
(ix) to present all stages of the review in the final report to enable critical appraisal and replication.

Definition and origin of systematic reviews

Research synthesis is *secondary research*. It involves techniques and strategies to accumulate the findings of *primary research* (Davies, Nutley, Smith 2000). Systematic reviews and meta-analyses are key features of research synthesis. They involve the search for, location, quality appraisal and narrative synthesis of all the relevant studies in a field. Meta-analysis involves the computation of a combined 'effect size' across the studies in a given field (Davies, Nutley, Smith 2000). Useful definitions of 'systematic review' and 'meta-analysis' are quoted in Chalmers *et al.* 2002:

> SYSTEMATIC REVIEW The application of strategies that limit bias in the assembly, critical appraisal, and synthesis of all relevant studies on a specific topic. Meta-analysis may be, but is not necessarily, used as part of this process. (pp. 176–7)
>
> META-ANALYSIS The statistical synthesis of the data from separate but similar, i.e. comparable studies, leading to a quantitative summary of the pooled results. (p. 14) (Last, 2001, *Dictionary of Epidemiology*, quoted in Chalmers *et al.* 2002)

There is a long history of the use of systematic review techniques in educational research to search for, retrieve and synthesize literature in a number of different contexts (Slavin 1986, Lipsey and Wilson 1993, Davies 2000, Petrosino *et al.* 2000). Educational researchers were among the early users of systematic reviews, although astronomers claim to be the first group of researchers to use the method (Slavin 1986, Petticrew 2001). Recently, Chalmers *et al.* (2002) have described a 'long history' of research synthesis in various disciplines and diverse subjects: medicine (i.e. treatments for scurvy in the eighteenth century), agriculture (also the eighteenth century), astronomy, and the 'psychology of time' (nineteenth century). The 'science of research synthesis' emerged in the twentieth century with Pearson's 1904 review of evidence on the effects of a vaccine against typhoid and some early reviews in the field of educational research (Chalmers *et al.* 2002). Educational researchers started combining the results of educational experiments in the first half of the twentieth century. In the 1950s and 1960s social science researchers explored different statistical approaches for undertaking meta-analyses. This was particularly so in the fields of education and psychology (Chalmers *et al.* 2002). Social scientists published many texts in the 1970s and 1980s on statistical approaches to meta-analysis and data synthesis (Glass 1976, Lipsey and Wilson 2001). It was only in relatively recent times that 'modern' health care researchers realized the merits of undertaking systematic reviews – although, as Chalmers *et al.* (2000) point out, James Lind performed a systematic review on treatments for scurvy in the eighteenth century. Certainly, it is only since the mid-1980s that there has been an explosion of systematic reviewing in health care.

Although educational researchers have undertaken 'research synthesis' for some considerable time (Slavin 1986) the term 'systematic review', however, is a relatively recent one and was initially used in health care research.

Traditionally, educational reviewers have used terms such as 'meta-analysis' and/or 'research synthesis' (Slavin 1986). The term 'meta-analysis' has a specific statistical meaning. It is a method of combining a number of quantitative studies in order to produce a more precise estimate of effect than can be achieved by any single study. It is not always the case that meta-analyses are undertaken on studies that have been identified using systematic review methods. Often it is not possible to combine studies statistically, and the synthesis of the findings of a range of quantitative studies can be done in other ways. Even when studies can be statistically combined this may not be appropriate. Slavin (1986) criticized educational researchers for combining all quantitative studies into a meta-analysis without due regard to their quality or context. He argued for a 'best-evidence synthesis' approach, whereby studies of certain quality and or contextual criteria are included within a meta-analysis. While the term 'research synthesis' moves the reviewer away from the requirement to undertake a meta-analysis of all identified studies it still implies some form of 'pooling' or meta-analysis of the data extracted from identified studies. Often this is simply not possible. Some studies, for example, may report no outcome data, which precludes their inclusion within a meta-analysis. Nevertheless, identification and reporting of the existence of these studies can be valuable, even if their results cannot be synthesized in quantitative ways. The systematic review process differs from meta-analysis and research synthesis in that it describes the whole process of identifying all the relevant literature within a given area.

Criticisms of systematic reviews

There have been a number of attacks on the rationale of systematic reviews (see for example, Pirrie 2001). The methodology of systematic reviews has been criticized because it is founded on 'questionable' premises about the nature of reviewing and ideas about research (see in particular, Hammersley 2001). Eysenck (1995) has criticized the 'mechanical' nature of the review process without sufficient regard to the quality and interpretation of the data.

There has been scepticism about the utility of systematic review methodology outside reviews of health care interventions using quantitative research designs. Conversely the relevance of the 'medical model' of research synthesis (based on the randomized controlled trial) to education has been questioned (Constable and Coe 2000, Pring 2000, Evans and Benefield 2001, Hammersley 2001).

Whilst many of the criticisms of systematic reviews have some merit, the alternative to a systematic review is bleaker: a narrative review with selection of studies based on the possible biases of the author. A more helpful approach to criticizing the conduct of systematic reviews is provided by Slavin (1986). Slavin has made similar points to Eysenck, in suggesting that some meta-analyses include all manner of quantitative studies – the 'good, bad and indifferent' (Eysenck 1995). Nevertheless, Slavin argues that the best-evidence synthesis approach (systematic review) that includes some aspect of quality appraisal moves us away from the unthinking mechanical nature of meta-analysis criticized by Eysenck, although this approach does reintroduce an element of 'subjectivity'.

Systematic reviewing is not 'value free'

Although the methods of a systematic review are firmly based within the 'positivist' tradition it is not a 'value free' approach. Early educational meta-analyses sought to avoid imposing the values of the researcher on the evidence by including all quantitative data in the review on the basis that bias can be introduced through the process of choosing to exclude certain studies (Slavin 1986). This procedure, however, can introduce bias by allowing poor-quality studies to influence the outcome. Slavin (1986) cogently argued that some form of judgement must be used to avoid introducing bias into the review from irrelevant or poor-quality studies. Thus, features of the systematic review method include value judgements throughout the process. These values include an explicit statement of the nature of the data that will be extracted from the included papers and details of the assumptions underpinning the basis on which the reviewer will interpret the included papers. The reviewer's values are implicit at each stage of the review, from the initial searches until the final synthesis. They are implicit in the choice of key terms employed in the searches, in the inclusion and exclusion criteria selected by the reviewer, and they are present in the interpretation of the included papers. Because the procedures in a systematic review are explicit and transparent the values used to inform the review are open to criticism, comment and consequent change by other reviewers. A systematic review of trials in health care suggested that routine administration of human albumin after large amounts of fluid loss, usually due to burn injuries, was associated with *increased* mortality (Cochrane Injuries Group Albumin Reviewers 1998, Roberts 2000). The findings of this review were contested by Wilkes and Navickis, who researched the literature using different inclusion criteria and did not find the alarming increase in mortality observed by Roberts and colleagues (Wilkes and Navickis 2001). Gough and Elbourne (2002) have characterized the process of undertaking a review as 'interpretive' rather than 'mechanical'. Whilst a systematic review approach can reduce some biases it is not, therefore, a value-free enterprise.

Systematic reviews for an 'evidence-informed society'

It is important that policy-makers, teachers and other educational stakeholders have access to the full range of 'evidence' on a subject in order to engage in the 'democratic debate' (Gough and Elbourne 2002) or participate in an 'evidence-informed society' (Young *et al.* 2002). This is the crux of the significance of systematic reviews: they can inform the development of a dynamic relationship between research, policy and practice. Research synthesis can also illuminate the field for future researchers by highlighting the problems of undertaking a study in a particular context. A systematic review may identify any existing relevant high-quality research, which might render redundant the requirement for more primary research (although sometimes research may be required to define the optimum dissemination and implementation strategies). A systematic review can help to inform the design of proposed research studies by giving estimates of effect sizes, which can be used to inform design issues such as sample size calculations. For example, a recent trial randomized 145 students on the basis that this would detect a difference of 0.43 of an effect size (Fukkink 2002); this difference was based on the findings of a previous systematic review. A systematic review can also help to inform the research question.

An interesting example of how systematic reviews informed both research and policy relates to the effect of class sizes on educational outcome. Meta-analyses of early experimental studies on the effect of class sizes on educational achievement indicated a small, but beneficial, effect of reducing class size on measures of achievement (Hedges 2000). These data, however, were criticized from a number of aspects. The studies tended to be small, localized and short-term, and whether the beneficial effect of reducing class size could be sustained to the general school population remained in doubt. In the 1990s a very large randomized trial undertaken in the state of Tennessee (USA) finally resolved the issue of class size. Children and teachers from 79 elementary schools were randomized to either be taught in or teach classes with a size of about fifteen children compared with classes of 25. The results of the trial confirmed both the beneficial effect of reducing class size and also that this benefit was sustained for several years (Hedges 2000). The results from this very large experiment were very similar to the earlier meta-analyses of small trials. This is an unusual example, in education, of the results of a systematic review of small trials being confirmed by the 'gold-standard' method: the large or mega trial.

Systematic reviews can also examine the external validity or generalizability of randomized trials. Many trials are undertaken in settings that are unlike 'normal' educational practice, for example within a university psychology department with psychologists or educational researchers delivering the intervention. Whether the effectiveness of such an intervention is applicable to a routine educational setting is open to debate. Fukkink (2002) observed, in a re-analysis of a systematic review, that an intervention delivered by researchers tended to have larger effects than when it was delivered in an ordinary school setting. By identifying all the relevant studies a systematic review can compensate for the poor external validity of a single experiment.

Effectiveness research

Both the Cochrane and Campbell Collaborations focus their attention, primarily, on identifying and synthesizing experimental and quasi-experimental research (Petrosino *et al.* 2000) because their priority is on issues of 'effectiveness', i.e. what works in interventions in health care, social policy, criminal justice and education. Experimental research is the most appropriate evidence of effectiveness in social research (Oakley 2000), and systematic reviews of randomized controlled trials and controlled trials are necessary in order to establish the effectiveness of an educational intervention (Petrosino *et al.* 2000, Gough and Elbourne 2002). In Chapter 2, the importance of experimental methods in educational research and the development of what has become by consensus the 'gold-standard' experimental method, the randomized controlled trial (RCT), are considered.

Summary

- There is an increasingly high profile of 'evidence-based' policy in education and the social sciences.
- A key element of this development is a renewed focus on the rationale and techniques of systematic reviewing.
- The stages of a systematic review aim to limit potential selection, publication and other biases.
- Systematic reviews can inform policy, practice and research.

2

The Nature of Evidence in Effectiveness Research

Educational research in the UK in the last 30 years has been dominated by the qualitative paradigm. Whilst qualitative research can give us important clues as to how and why something may or may not work, can prefigure and clarify issues in a particular field of enquiry and, on occasions, be a useful supplement to quantitative research, it cannot tell us whether or not an educational intervention is actually effective. This requires testing using an experimental or quasi-experimental research design where at least two groups are compared: one receiving the educational intervention under evaluation, the other acting as a control.

Controlled evaluations have been used, intermittently, for many centuries. Chalmers reports several examples of controlled trials of medical treatments, including the famous Lind study of citrus fruits for the treatment of scurvy in the mid-eighteenth century and an evaluation of bleeding among sick soldiers in the Peninsular War at the beginning of the nineteenth century (Chalmers *et al.* 2002). Controlled evaluations increased substantially in the twentieth century. The medical community celebrates the 1948 MRC Streptomycin trial that is generally believed to be the first 'true' randomized trial. Oakley claims that educational and psychological randomized trials pre-date the Streptomycin trial by up to 50 years (1998, 2000). Chalmers, however, whilst acknowledging the existence of relatively robust quasi-randomized experiments, has found no strong evidence that a 'true' controlled trial using random allocation was performed before the 1948 MRC Streptomycin trial (Chalmers, personal communication, 2001). Nevertheless, there are some important 'classical' quasi-experimental studies undertaken before 1948 that underpin the need for rigorous experimental methodology.

The Cambridge-Somerfield experiment (Oakley 2000) undertaken in 1937 allocated 160 'delinquent' boys to either receive social worker support or to act as controls. Teachers were asked to identify boys at risk, and about 160 boys were randomized to be controls or to receive extended pastoral care. The results indicated no evidence of benefit of the intervention; indeed, there was evidence of harm. In the last follow-up in 1975 42 per cent of the boys in the intervention group had had an undesirable outcome (e.g. criminal conviction, early death, etc.) compared with 32 per cent of the boys in the control group. This was a statistically significant difference. The results of this trial appeared to demonstrate a harmful effect of social workers for such boys. In this instance, an experiment demonstrated that an intervention that was widely believed to 'help' children was actually harmful.

More recently a systematic review of experimental studies of 'scared straight', a method used widely in the USA and, occasionally, in the UK, showed that this intervention to prevent adolescents from turning to crime actually increased criminal activity (Petrosino *et al.* 2002). The dissemination of 'scared straight' was based upon anecdotal evidence that taking juvenile petty offenders to be 'scared' by hardened incarcerated criminals would persuade them not to reoffend. A systematic review of randomized controlled trials, however, showed it had the opposite effect.

In the early 1970s US educational researchers persuaded head teachers and the Federal Government to allow schools with large numbers of African-American pupils, from poor areas, to be randomized to either receive an added financial injection or to act as a control (Crain and York 1976). There was opposition to the experiment, partly to enable grounds that the amount of money was too small in order a difference to be demonstrated. However, because randomization controlled for confounding factors, the experiment *did* show that the children's test scores significantly improved compared with similar children in control schools. This result persuaded policy-makers to offer similar financial packages to other schools in deprived areas.

In the 1990s a large field trial of small class size was undertaken in Tennessee (costing approximately $12 million) showing the benefit of smaller class sizes (Hedges 2000).

Many of the early educational experiments did not use 'true' randomization. Rather, they used quasi-random methods to form groups. A common method is alternation. Alternation might take the form of allocating all children with a surname starting with A to one group whilst all children with a surname beginning with B are allocated to another group. This method, however, can lead to the formation of biased groups and is generally now being replaced by true random allocation.

There have been numerous RCTs in social and educational research (Petrosino *et al.* 2000), but this research paradigm has received less attention in the past 30 years partly as it has appeared to be the 'loser' in the 30-year paradigm war (Oakley 1998). Recently it has come to the attention of policy-makers that inferences about what does and does not work in education cannot be drawn either from qualitative research or quantitative research of an observational nature. Boruch (1994) notes, in the USA at least, an increase in the use of RCTs in the social sciences, and looks forward to the day when, if at all possible, social science interventions will be evaluated using the RCT. Absence of controlled tests in an area leads to a debate among the 'ignorant' (Boruch 1994).

Randomized controlled trials

The most robust method of assessing whether something is effective or not is the randomized controlled trial (RCT). Cook (2002) has argued that in health and social policy the RCT has long been recognized as the most rigorous method of estimating effectiveness. As far back as the 1920s educational researchers were describing how to experiment in education using a randomly formed control group (Oakley 1998). As with systematic reviews, educational researchers were in the forefront of the design of controlled experiments. More recently, many educational researchers have viewed the RCT as a design that is either not possible to undertake in educational research, or is from an inappropriate paradigm. It is not the intention to explore these issues in this book: they have been well documented elsewhere (see for example, Oakley 2000).

In an RCT participants are randomly allocated to the interventions being evaluated. Typically, a participant will be allocated either to the new intervention (the so-called experimental group) or allocated to whatever is the usual practice (the control group). There are many variants to this design, for example allocating the participants to receive the new intervention either straight away or later (a waiting list design), or to receive both the new and the old intervention but in different randomized sequences (reversal or cross-over design), or allocating groups (in educational research this is usually intact classes or schools) in a cluster design. However, the essence of this design and all its variants is the *random* allocation. If participants are allocated on any other basis, one cannot be sure whether (except for chance differences) the experimental and control groups were similar before receiving (or not receiving) the intervention, and therefore it becomes impossible to disentangle the effects of the intervention from the characteristics of the people being allocated to the intervention. Techniques can be used to attempt to control for the potential confounding from known variables, but they cannot adjust for unknown variables.

Why randomization?

There are a number of methods of assembling two or more groups for the purposes of comparing whether an intervention is effective or not. The benefits of using random allocation have been described previously (e.g. Cook and Campbell 1979, Torgerson and Torgerson 2001, Torgerson and Torgerson 2003a). It is not proposed to detail the design and strengths of RCTs; however, it is important to discuss their main features in order to be able to distinguish between high- and low-quality RCTs. The two main reasons for using random allocation are to avoid regression to the mean effects and selection bias. Randomization avoids both of these problems; however, selection bias in particular can be introduced after random allocation in poor-quality trials.

Regression to the mean

Regression to the mean (RTM) is a highly prevalent problem that affects most areas of human endeavour. In education it is a particularly severe problem affecting areas such as students' test scores and school league tables. The phenomenon occurs when a variable is measured on one occasion and then is remeasured subsequently. This phenomenon explains why researchers consider the pre- and post-test 'quasi-experiment' the weakest research design (Cook and Campbell 1979). In a pre- and post-test evaluation typically students are selected who have scores that are below some threshold: that is they are scoring badly. If we retest such students then the 'average' mark will move upwards irrespective of any intervention. If there is an intervention the improvement due to the regression to the mean phenomenon may be erroneously ascribed to the intervention. A review of pre- and post-test studies by Lipsey and Wilson (1993) showed that such studies produce effect sizes with an average 61 per cent greater improvement than studies that use a control group. Part of this exaggerated benefit is almost certainly due to regression to the mean. Forming comparison groups using random allocation deals with regression to the mean as it affects both groups equally and the effect is 'cancelled out' in the comparison between the post-test means.

Selection bias

Selection bias occurs when the groups formed for comparison have not been created through random allocation and are different in some way that can affect outcome. Schools who volunteer to pilot a change in the curriculum will often be different from schools that do not volunteer. Comparing these two groups of schools will be susceptible to 'confounding' as there is likely to be some characteristic present in one group of schools that could explain differences in outcomes. Similarly, individuals who volunteer or ask to take part in an intervention are likely to differ in some way from those who do not. Such differences could again explain any differences in outcome.

Systematic reviews of randomized trials

In an ideal world, evidence-based policy and practice in education for questions of effectiveness should be informed through systematic reviews of the results of large, well-conducted, randomized controlled trials. In areas where there are RCTs these often tend to be relatively small. Which reduces the possibility of an individual trial giving a clear and unambiguous answer. Systematic review methods are particularly valuable when the field of inquiry contains large numbers of relatively small randomized trials as is so often the case in educational research. When small randomized trials are examined on an individual basis they can give misleading results. This is because they have relatively low statistical power to detect modest but important differences in educationally important outcomes. By using meta-analytical methods similar trials can be pooled to enable the analyst to observe, as statistically significant, worthwhile effect sizes that individual trials may have missed.

Whilst meta-analysis can go some way towards addressing the problem of underpowered trials, it will not produce a true estimate of effectiveness if the trials contained within the analysis are methodologically flawed. In addition, meta-analyses may give unduly optimistic results if there is substantial publication bias, that is if studies that show either a null or negative effect remain unpublished and therefore cannot be included in any form of review. The issue of trials with poor or flawed methodology can be addressed in a systematic review through the use of inclusion and or exclusion criteria. In terms of the problems of publication bias, if the studies cannot be identified then they cannot be included, no matter how exhaustive the review. There are techniques, however, that can be used to identify whether or not for a given review there is a danger of publication bias. This problem and the issue of trial quality will be addressed later.

Because the need to know whether something works or not should be the overarching aim of any body of research, this book makes no apology for the decision to focus solely on procedures for undertaking systematic reviews of randomized controlled trials.

Summary

- Experimental research is essential in questions of effectiveness.
- There is a 'long history' of experimental research in education and the social sciences.
- The most robust method of assessing effectiveness is the randomized controlled trial (RCT).
- Systematic reviews and meta-analyses of RCTs are valuable research tools.

3

The Stages of a Systematic Review

The stages of a systematic review are well established in health care (for example, Egger and Davey-Smith 2001, NHS Centre for Reviews and Dissemination 2001), in social policy (Oakley 2002) and in education (for example, Badger *et al.* 2000, Evans and Benefield 2001):

(i) A *protocol* or plan of the research is written to establish: the theoretical, empirical and conceptual background to the review; the research question(s); the objectives; the scope of the review and the methods for searching, screening, data extraction, quality appraisal and synthesis.

(ii) Within the protocol a set of predetermined written *inclusion and exclusion criteria* are specified. For example, the protocol may specify that only studies employing a 'true experimental' design and written in the English language will be included.

(iii) Once the protocol has been developed and, ideally, peer reviewed, the *literature search* can commence, starting with an electronic search. The literature search may also include hand searching of key journals and other methods of retrieval. The results of the search are then *screened* by at least two independent reviewers, firstly on the basis of titles and abstracts (first stage screening), and secondly on the basis of full papers (second stage screening).

(iv) At the '*scoping*' or '*mapping*' stage the studies retrieved for the review are described and classified. At this stage all of these studies may be data extracted for inclusion in the *in-depth review*, or it may be decided to further refine the research question and inclusion criteria and select a more narrowly focused area for the full systematic review.

(v) Once relevant papers have been identified their data need to be extracted, using a standard data extraction sheet, again using at least two independent researchers (*double data extraction*). Also the studies are assessed to determine their quality (*quality appraisal*). This is usually based on internal validity, but includes some analysis of external validity.

(vi) Extracted data are then summarized in a *synthesis*. This can be done as a 'qualitative' overview if the data are not in a form that permits a statistical summary. If the data are numerical and are of sufficient homogeneity then they can be combined within a *meta-analysis*, which will give an overall figure for the effect of an intervention.

(vii) Finally, the synthesized data will be interpreted within a *report*, which should be exposed to peer-review before publication.

Summary

- The seven main stages of a systematic review are well established in health care, social policy and educational research.
- The stages include: writing the protocol (including the inclusion and exclusion criteria); searching and screening; 'scoping' or 'mapping' the research; extracting data from the included studies and quality appraising them; synthesizing the studies in a narrative, and sometimes in a meta-analysis; writing and disseminating the report.

4

Developing a Protocol; Searching and Screening; Data Extraction

Developing a protocol

The first stage in a systematic review is the development of the review protocol. The protocol is an *a priori* statement of the aims and methods of the review. The idea behind writing a review protocol is that the research question(s), the aims and the methods of the review are considered in advance of identifying the relevant literature. This allows the reviewer to conduct the review with minimal bias, and ensures greater efficiency in the review process. Stating a clear research question before the literature search is undertaken will prevent unnecessary effort and cost in identifying and retrieving irrelevant papers. The criteria for including papers in the systematic review are established *a priori*, in order to reduce the possibility of reviewer selection and inclusion bias, by avoiding the situation where criteria are changed as the review progresses or decisions are made to include studies on the basis of their results. If the decisions are explicit this enables them to be justified. The rationale for developing the protocol as independently as possible from the literature is that this avoids the research question and the inclusion/exclusion criteria being unduly influenced by one or two studies, which can lead to bias. For example, if reviewers are aware of the existence of 'seminal' studies in the area, they may develop their research question and inclusion criteria to ensure that these particular studies are included. The known studies, for example, may have used non-random allocation processes and would have been excluded if the inclusion criteria specified randomized trials. The reviewers, however, may be tempted to specify inclusion criteria that include 'quasi-random' and controlled trials as well as randomized trials, simply in order to include the known studies.

Previous guidance for systematic reviews in health care can be contradictory. For example, Egger and Davey-Smith (2001), whilst recommending the writing of an *a priori* review protocol, also state that:

> The review protocol should ideally be conceived by a group of reviewers with expertise both in the *content area* and the science of research synthesis. (Egger and Davey-Smith 2001, emphasis added)

Involving content experts in the review will necessarily include viewpoints already 'influenced' by non-systematic knowledge of existing research studies. Therefore, it is often not possible for a researcher to be truly unfamiliar with all the relevant studies. Knowledge of at least some of the existing studies is almost certainly going to influence the protocol. Indeed, it could be argued that a preliminary literature review should be used to influence and refine the protocol. A cursory electronic search (*rapid scope*) can be used to estimate the size of the relevant literature. For instance, a rapid scope of the literature on the effects on reading and spelling of interventions to increase phonemic awareness would reveal large numbers (50 to 60) of experimental studies conducted in the USA in the last 20 to 30 years (Ehri, Nunes, Stahl, Willows 2001). If the review resources are scarce (e.g. a student undertaking a review for a thesis) then it might not be possible to review all the relevant literature in this vast field. An alternative approach might be to develop a protocol that defines a very narrow research question (e.g. the effect of phonemic awareness training on the development of beginning reading, in 'normally achieving' children aged 4 to 6: this is a relatively small literature).

A scoping review is also important in order to identify existing systematic reviews in the area. If the scoping review uncovers a recent, rigorous review within the area that already addresses the proposed research question it would be unnecessary to repeat the review. In this situation the research question could be refined to address another policy relevant question.

Expert knowledge of a number of existing studies, particularly if they tend to be obscure references, may be helpful in developing the electronic search strategy. An exhaustive strategy ought to identify all known, relevant, papers as well as ones that are unknown. Prior knowledge of an area, therefore, can aid the review process, although the reviewer must be aware that it can also introduce bias to the review. The latter problem can be reduced if clear, consistent and logical justifications are made for the inclusion criteria.

Conceptual issues central to the review should be firmly embedded in the protocol. For example, in systematic reviews of literacy learning the relevant conceptual issues might include the nature of literacy, learner characteristics, literacy outcomes or measures and the nature of the interventions. The conceptual issues will help the reviewers to refine their research question for the review to make it well focused and relevant.

In a high-quality systematic review the inclusion and exclusion criteria are rigorously and transparently reported. The inclusion and exclusion criteria will include the time span of publications, the type of research to be reviewed (study design) and the relevance to the research question.

The protocol will also include criteria for quality appraising the included studies (e.g. CONSORT guidelines, Altman 1996), and the categories for data extraction will be specified. In addition, it can be stated that in the eventual synthesis of the research, more weight will be given to the studies assessed as being of 'higher quality'.

The key features of the application of the inclusion and exclusion criteria are:

- they are established *a priori*;
- they are explicit;
- they are applied stringently;
- all studies retrieved from the searches are listed in tables at the end of the report (together with reasons justifying inclusion and exclusion).

It is helpful to set out the review protocol in a consistent format, which will aid peer reviewers. As an example, a protocol for a systematic review of randomized trials evaluating interventions in the teaching of spelling is shown in Box 4.1.

Box 4.1 Example of a review protocol

What is the title?
A systematic review and meta-analysis of randomized controlled trials evaluating interventions in the teaching of spelling.

What is the context and what are the conceptual issues?
There is a widespread consensus that spelling is a difficult skill. Indeed, some believe it to be more difficult than reading, because it requires the formation of an exact sequence of letters without any contextual clues (Fulk and Stormont-Spurgin 1995). Poor spelling skills are a widespread problem. Many children find spelling difficult, particularly those who experience learning difficulties (Fulk and Stormont-Spurgin 1995),

but including those who are high attainers in other areas (McClurg and Kasakow 1989). Many children continue to rely on phonetic strategies into their later years, and there is still controversy among teachers and researchers about the appropriate strategies for spelling instruction (McClurg and Kasakow 1989). Whilst spelling is often seen as a 'lower order' literacy skill based on memory, this view is simplistic: it is a highly complex ability.

Spelling acquisition, like other aspects of literacy, is developmental. Teachers use a variety of methods and instructional techniques to teach spelling skills, for example systematic study or structured study conditions, multisensory training, and spelling within the context of written composition. It is often unclear which is the most effective method of teaching spelling. Consequently most teachers use a variety of methods.

What is the policy context?

In the UK, The National Literacy Strategy for England and Wales gives detailed guidance for teaching and learning spelling (DfEE 1998). In the early years and throughout Key Stage 1 the emphasis is on phonological awareness, phonemic awareness and phonics teaching. At Key Stage 2 the emphasis for spelling is on individual self-correction strategies, independent spelling strategies (for example, phonics-based strategies, dictionaries and IT spell-checks), learning spelling conventions and rules (for example, patterns, prefixes and suffixes), practising spelling (using 'look, say, cover, write, check') and investigating the spelling of words (for example, word origins and derivations). Although the strategy is still highly contested, clearly it follows the now uncontested developmental model of spelling abilities. At Key Stage 1 the influence of international research synthesis on phonological awareness training, phonemic awareness training and systematic phonics teaching is evident (Troia 1999, Ehri, Nunes, Stahl, Willows 2001, Ehri, Nunes, Willows *et al.* 2001).

Has a scoping review been undertaken (if yes, what were the results)?

A scoping review was undertaken which found six relevant systematic reviews (Fulk and Stormont-Spurgin 1995, Troia

1999, MacArthur *et al.* 2001, Ehri, Nunes, Stahl, Willows 2001, Ehri, Nunes, Willows *et al.* 2001, Torgerson and Elbourne 2002). Two examined the effect of ICT on spelling acquisition (MacArthur *et al.* 2001, Torgerson and Elbourne 2002). The third review investigated phonological awareness training (Troia 1999); the fourth examined the effect of phonemic awareness training (Ehri, Nunes, Stahl, Willows 2001); the fifth systematically reviewed the experimental research on systematic phonics teaching versus non-systematic phonics teaching and the sixth reviewed published research on spelling interventions designed for pupils experiencing learning disabilities (Fulk and Stormont-Spurgin 1995).

What is the aim?
This aim of this review is to help fill the gap in the knowledge base of what does and does not work in the teaching of spelling.

What is the research question?
The research question for the scoping stage of the review is: which interventions or strategies are effective in the teaching of spelling for pupils aged between 5 and 16? The research question for the in-depth stage of the review is: which interventions or strategies are effective in the teaching of spelling for 'normally achieving' pupils aged between 7 and 14 (in the UK, Key Stage 2). The reason for limiting the review in this way at the in-depth stage is because of the existence of previous systematic reviews in early literacy development (Troia 1999, Ehri, Nunes, Stahl, Willows 2001, Ehri, Nunes, Willows *et al.* 2001) and spelling development with children experiencing learning disabilities (Fulk and Stormont-Spurgin 1995), and the lack of a systematic review focusing on interventions to improve the spelling abilities of 'normally achieving' children and young people aged between 7 and 14 (in the UK, Key Stage 2).

What is the search strategy?
The Educational Resources Information Center (ERIC); PsycINFO; and The Campbell Collaboration Social, Psychological, Educational Criminological Trials Register (C2 SPECTR) will be searched. All the searches will be for the

period 1980–2002. As the topic focus will be the teaching of the spelling of English, the search will be restricted to the English language research literature. In a previous review of ICT and spelling (Torgerson and Elbourne 2002) it was found that the key words of allocat* experiment* and random* was the most sensitive search strategy for the identification of trials. These key words combined with spell*, should be the most sensitive search strategy for this review.

What are the inclusion/exclusion criteria?
As the research question is looking at 'effectiveness', papers using rigorous methods to assess effectiveness will be required. In essence, this implies randomized controlled trials (RCTs). Therefore, only randomized controlled trials (or systematic reviews containing at least one RCT) will be eligible for inclusion. For a paper to be included it will have to be a trial comparing two or more methods or strategies for the teaching and/or learning of spelling in a school setting. RCTs will only be included if they are undertaken in English-speaking countries, and written in the English language. Trials will be included if they are published (or unpublished but in the public domain) in the years 1980–2003 and if all of the participants are aged between 5 and 16. To be included in the review a trial will have to report at least one spelling outcome measure.

How will the data be extracted and analysed?
Data about participants, interventions, outcomes and quality of the studies will be extracted from all the included papers, using a standard format. Included studies will be tabulated, and effect sizes for the main and secondary outcomes will be calculated. Standardized effect sizes will be estimated by dividing the mean differences between the groups by a pooled standard deviation using a commercially available software package.

The educational validity of pooling two or more of the trials in a meta-analysis will be estimated using expert opinion. If appropriate, trials with a similar contextual framework will be pooled in a meta-analysis. Statistical and educational sources of heterogeneity will be investigated and possible reasons described. Sensitivity analyses of the results will include country specific analysis as well as cross-national pooling, high- versus low-quality trials. Potential publication bias will be explored using a funnel plot and also comparing effect sizes from published and unpublished reports.

How will the quality of studies be assessed?
The trials will be quality appraised using a checklist derived from the CONSORT guidelines (Altman 1996). These guidelines are used by the major medical journals when publishing randomized controlled trials and include, for example, the following internal validity criteria: are groups comparable at baseline? was 'intention to teach' used? were post-tests undertaken 'blind'? The external validity of included trials will also be examined.

References

Altman, D. G. (1996) 'Better reporting of randomised controlled trials: the CONSORT statement', *British Medical Journal*, 313, 570–1.

DfEE (1989) *The National Literacy Strategy. Framework for Teaching*: London: DfEE.

Ehri, L. C., Nunes, S. R., Stahl, S. A. and Willows, D. M. (2001) 'Systematic phonics instruction helps students learn to read: evidence from the national reading panel's meta-analysis', *Review of Educational Research*, 71, 393–447.

Ehri, L. C., Nunes, S. R. and Willows, D. M., Valeska Schuster, B., Yaghoub-Zadeh, Z. and Shanahan, T. (2001) 'Phonemic awareness instruction helps children learn to read: evidence from the National Reading Panel's meta-analysis', *Reading Research Quarterly*, 36 (3), July/August/September 250–87.

Fulk, B. M. and Stormont-Spurgin, M. (1995) 'Spelling interventions for students with disabilities: a review', *The Journal of Special Education*, 28 (4), 488–513.

MacArthur, C. A., Ferretti, R. P., Okolo, C. M. and Cavalier, A. R. (2001) 'Technology applications for students with literacy problems: a critical review', *The Elementary School Journal*, 101 (3), 273–301.

McClurg, P. A. and Kasakow, N. (1989) 'Wordprocessors, spelling checkers, and drill and practice programs: effective tools for spelling instruction?', *Journal of Educational Computing Research*, 5, 187–98.

Torgerson, C. J. and Elbourne, D. (2002) 'A systematic review and meta-analysis of the effectiveness of information and communication technology (ICT) on the teaching of spelling', *Journal of Research in Reading*, 35 (2), 129–43.
Troia, G. A. (1999) 'Phonological awareness intervention research: a critical review of the experimental methodology', *Reading Research Quarterly*, 34, 28–52.

The review protocol is an important first step when undertaking a systematic review. It helps to focus and structure the review; it limits the scope for bias occurring in the review and enables an independent third party to critically appraise the finished review in relation to the initial proposal.

Literature search

The main thrust of the search should be in the electronic databases, as being the most efficient method of retrieval (NHS Centre for Reviews and Dissemination 2001). This is mainly due to the technological explosion in the last ten to fifteen years and the subsequent availability of educational and other relevant electronic databases that can be systematically searched. However, there are many other sources of educational studies: key journals; the bibliographies of systematic and other reviews; websites; personal contact with content specialists. Whilst using all of the above methods for retrieval may make the search more exhaustive, some of the methods can increase the risk of potential selection bias. This problem is discussed below.

The three methods that are least liable to selection bias are searching electronic databases, hand searching of key journals and searching the bibliographies of previous systematic reviews, because all of these methods employ a 'systematic' approach. Therefore this book will confine itself to an overview of how randomized trials might be identified using these three methods.

Ideally before undertaking a search of electronic databases it is extremely helpful to enlist the aid of a librarian or information specialist who will know how to access the most relevant databases and will be able to advise on the appropriate search strategy for each database.

Electronic searching

A preliminary search of the main electronic databases often takes place to aid the development of the review protocol (rapid scope). Health care reviewers, who are focusing only on randomized controlled trials, are in the fortunate position of being able to search a single database (the Cochrane Library) that contains all RCTs relating to health. Presently, educational and other non-health care reviewers are less fortunate. In future the Campbell Library may rival the Cochrane Library in its completeness but this is not the case at present. In addition, the EPPI-Centre is developing an electronic database of reviews in educational research. At present, however, the educational researcher must search across a number of electronic databases to ensure that the majority of RCTs within a given area are identified.

For any search strategy there is a trade-off between 'sensitivity' and 'specificity'. A search strategy that is extremely sensitive is likely to include as many of the relevant studies as possible that are present on a database. Clearly the most sensitive strategy is a search of the entire database. Specificity relates to the concept of 'homing' in on the most relevant papers. Any search strategy that does not involve screening the entire database introduces specificity. The trade-off between sensitivity and specificity begins as soon as terms are introduced that start to exclude studies. It is absolutely essential to introduce search terms to reduce the huge volume of literature within the educational databases. However, even the most specific search strategy will reveal many papers that could be RCTs and the only way to ascertain whether they are or not is to retrieve them and check in the methods section what the researchers actually did.

Designing the search strategy

The use of the 'wildcard' characters * and $ is important for devising appropriate research terms. Studies using random allocation may keyword this in numerous ways in the title or abstract. For example, a study might state: 'we undertook a randomized trial' (with either 's' or 'z'); or 'we randomly placed'; or 'we performed random allocation'; or 'groups were formed by using random number tables'. Rather than trying all the different methods of using the word 'random' a search term with random* will identify all the words with the stem random. Educational and psychological databases actually do not often use the term random* when describing randomized controlled trials. A widely used word is 'experiment' or 'experimental' with the term experiment* being appropriate for the search. Many researchers in the educational field seem to be rather hesitant about describing their study as a trial or an experiment and sometimes they will state in the abstract that participants were 'allocated into two groups'. Often in such studies true randomization has occurred but this is only apparent when the full paper is retrieved and the methods section scrutinized. Therefore, the term allocat* should also be used to identify studies which contain 'allocate', 'allocation' and 'allocated' in their title and abstract. A search term using the phrase 'allocat* or experiment* or random*' should include most of the experimental studies from an educational database.

The Campbell Collaboration has developed a search strategy that helps identify controlled trials within the educational databases (see Petrosino *et al.* 2000, Appendix 1).

Where are the randomized controlled trials in educational research?

There are a number of electronic databases that can be used to search for randomized controlled trials. These include PsycINFO (a database of psychological literature); ERIC (Educational Resources Information Center); BEI (British Educational Index); C2-SPECTR (Campbell Collaboration Social, Psychological, Educational and Criminal Trials Register) and SSCI (Social Sciences Citation Index). In addition, the database of 'grey' literature (i.e. unpublished literature in the public domain, e.g. reports, theses) can be searched (System for Information on Grey Literature in Europe: SIGLE), although ERIC is also a good source for this kind of literature.

Each of these databases has its strengths and weaknesses. With respect to searching for randomized controlled trials PsycINFO and ERIC are, at present, the richest sources of controlled studies for most educational reviews. However, as stated previously, the establishment of the Campbell Collaboration may change this situation in the future.

As an example, consider the findings of two recent systematic reviews: one reviewing research on the effectiveness of information and communication technology on literacy (Torgerson and Zhu 2003), and a systematic review of interventions to increase adult literacy and numeracy (Torgerson, Porthouse, Brooks 2003). These two reviews contained a total of 51 RCTs: 42 RCTs in the review of ICT and literacy and nine in the adult literacy and numeracy review. Table 4.1 shows the origin, by method of retrieval (electronic database or hand search) of all these RCTs.

Table 4.1 Origin of identified RCTs

Electronic database/hand search	Number of RCTs
PsycINFO	29
ERIC	16
SSCI	2
BEI	2
Hand search	2

Fifty-seven per cent of the RCTs were retrieved from PsycINFO with a further 31 per cent identified from ERIC. Together these two databases contained 88 per cent of all the RCTs identified for these two reviews. The other databases produced only a few additional references, as did hand searching of key journals. Nevertheless, if the search had been confined to PsycINFO and ERIC this would have led to the loss of more than a tenth of the relevant trials.

Hand searching

Because trials in educational research tend not to be specifically 'tagged' in educational databases, unlike their health equivalents, hand searching may be helpful in identifying some papers. The choice of journals to hand search should be based on which journals are most likely to yield the relevant trials. Sometimes the electronic searches can aid this decision by indicating which journals are the sources for most of the trials. Additionally, some journals, especially the newer ones, have not yet been indexed on the electronic databases and therefore the only way that relevant articles can be retrieved from these journals is through hand searching. Searching obscure journals can be challenging. If university libraries do not hold them, sometimes the only option is to spend time at a national library (e.g. in the UK the British Library in London or its lending division at Boston Spa in Yorkshire; in the US the Smithsonian Institute in Washington).

Searching reference lists of systematic reviews

Previous systematic reviews can be helpful in identifying relevant papers. Reviews that address similar research questions or include questions that overlap with the systematic review being undertaken may contain relevant references.

Sources of search bias

The searching process can be prone to bias. Many reviewers, for example, use 'personal knowledge' or 'personal contacts' to identify relevant studies. In theory this can result in bias if the same studies are not identified by electronic or hand searching. The problem with personal knowledge is that studies favouring a particular viewpoint are more likely to have been noted and retained whilst other studies not favouring this perspective may have been discarded. On the other hand, personal knowledge may reveal key unpublished trials, which if not included, could result in the review coming to erroneous conclusions. Therefore, it is not immediately clear whether such references should be included or not. A useful compromise is to include them but examine the results of the review when they are excluded (i.e. by undertaking a sensitivity analysis).

Some reviewers also search the bibliographies of non-systematic reviews as a means of identifying relevant studies. The problem with this is that non-systematic reviews may include a biased sample of the literature and this bias could then be introduced into the systematic review.

Screening

Once the search strategy has been determined, and potentially relevant titles and abstracts identified, the next step is to filter out the irrelevant papers and screen in possibly relevant articles. The first step in this process is to 'de-duplicate' the references by importing them into a reference management software package (e.g. EndNote; Pro-Cite; Reference Manager). Establishing a database of references enables a record to be kept of every step of the review, which if necessary can be rerun by a third party.

Potentially relevant studies are identified from titles and abstracts (first stage screening). Irrelevant papers are filtered out and potentially relevant papers are sent for. These are then read and identified as either being relevant or not (second stage screening). These processes are, ideally, undertaken by two independent researchers to ensure that only a minimal number of relevant studies are 'missed'. If reviewers agree on references these can be either discarded or retrieved. If there is disagreement the references can be examined by both reviewers and discussed, at which stage they can either be included or rejected. Double screening, however, is resource intensive. An alternative strategy is for the database to be screened by one reviewer only. A second reviewer can then screen a random sample of the database (e.g. 10 per cent). This random sample of citations can be used to measure the inter-rater reliability assessment of the agreement between the reviewers. The statistic, Cohen's Kappa, can then be calculated to measure how well the two raters agree. This takes into account the agreement that would have occurred by chance. The values range between +1 (perfect agreement) and 0. A value of 0 indicates that the observed agreement could have occurred by chance. This process describes how well the decisions could be reproduced.

Table 4.2 A worked example of inter-rater reliability assessment using Cohen's Kappa

	Screener B		
Screener A	Include	Exclude	Total
Include	85	60	145
Exclude	59	4320	4379
Total	144	4380	4524

If the level of agreement, as measured by Cohen's Kappa, is high (for example 0.90) then the results of the single reviewer can be relied upon. However, if agreement is low (for example 0.25), then it would be necessary for the second person to double screen all of the citations.

The process of calculating Cohen's Kappa is undertaken with reference to Table 4.2 as follows. An electronic screening strategy identified 4524 potential articles and two reviewers screened this database. To find out how well they agree the exact number of agreements is calculated, which in Table 4.2 is 85 + 4320 = 4405. From a total of 4524 articles this is 0.97 or 97 per cent (i.e. 4405/4524). This overall agreement figure, however, takes no account of the fact that some of the agreement will occur by chance. The next step is to take this chance effect into account.

Include	$144 \times 145/4524 =$	4.62
Exclude	$4379 \times 4380/4524 =$	4239.61
Total		4244.22

The number of agreements that is expected by chance, therefore, is 4244.22, which as a proportion of the total articles is 4244.22/4524 = 0.938. The maximum agreement is 1.0, therefore, we can calculate the inter-rater reliability agreement as:

$$\frac{0.97 - 0.938}{1.00 - 0.938}$$

which results in a Kappa value of 0.52 (moderate).

Table 4.3 presents the results of screening a search for relevant randomized controlled trials, controlled trials and reviews for a systematic review of interventions to increase adult literacy and/or numeracy (Torgerson, Porthouse, Brooks 2003). The number of relevant studies can be extremely small: about one-third of 1 per cent for RCTs in the case of this review. In this instance the database of 'Criminal Justice Abstracts' was searched because, although it is not an educational database, it was known that controlled trials had been undertaken in prison settings. Five CTs and reviews were retrieved from this database although none of these was a randomized controlled trial.

Table 4.4 is a 'scoping' or 'mapping' table, which shows the numbers of studies that were retrieved after screening of the electronic searches, and the reasons why only twelve of

Table 4.3 Origin of all included studies

	Found	Included RCTs, CTs and systematic and other reviews	Number of RCTs
ERIC	2628	40	9 (0.34%)
PsycINFO	971	3	2 (0.21%)
CJA	736	5	0
SSCI	15	2	2 (13%)
C2-SPECTR	8	1	0
SIGLE	172	1	0
Website	11	2	1 (9%)
Bibliography search	13	4	1 (8%)
Contact	1	1	0
Total	4555	59	15 (0.33%)

Table 4.4 Mapping of relevant RCTs, CTs and reviews

RCTs	12 papers (containing 9 trials)
RCTs (no results)	3
CTs	34
Reviews	10
Total	59

the 59 papers were deemed relevant for the in-depth review. Because the requirements of this review were to identify primarily RCTs but also controlled trials (CTs) both are listed in the mapping table, along with relevant review articles. However, because the inclusion criteria for this review specified including only RCTs in the in-depth review only nine RCTs (reported in twelve papers) were data extracted and quality appraised. The other papers (controlled trials and reviews) were used to provide conceptual background information.

In Tables 4.5 to 4.7 the process of screening and mapping the literature within a given field, in this case a systematic

Table 4.5 Screening and mapping of the literature in a systematic review on spelling

	Found and screened	Ex-first stage*	Sent for	Ex-second stage**	Not received	Included in map***	Included in in-depth
ERIC	178	131	47	31	1	15	3
PsycINFO	311	265	46	27	1	18	7
Expert contact	6	1	5	0	0	5	0
Bibliographic searches	3	0	3	0	1	2	1
Total	498	397	101	58	3	40	11

* Screening on the basis of titles and abstracts; all 'includes' sent for
** Screening on the basis of full papers received
*** Description of the research in the field

Table 4.6 Reasons for first and second stage exclusions

	First stage exclusions	Second stage exclusions
Not spelling	106	0
Not spelling intervention	27	8
Not English	52	5
Not trial	140	8
Age 1 (not 5–16)***	14	1
Not randomized controlled trial (or systematic review containing at least one RCT)	58	32
Not spelling only	0	4
Total	397	58

*** For scoping stage RCTs evaluating interventions in pupils aged between 5 and 16 were included

Table 4.7 Third stage exclusions (29 papers in the 'map' of the research, but excluded from the in-depth review)

Learning disabilities	10
Age 2 (not 7–14)**	12*
Reading disabilities	2
Reading	1
Systematic review	4
Total	29

* Two of these papers contain the same study

** For in-depth review only RCTs evaluating interventions in pupils aged between 7 and 14 (Key Stage 2) were included. This was because the in-depth review excluded early literacy interventions (phonological awareness and phonemic awareness training)

review of spelling interventions, is described. Table 4.5 shows the origin of the studies that were identified in the original electronic search. The original number of studies, 498, is reduced through a series of predefined exclusion criteria until only eleven relevant studies are left for the in-depth systematic review. Tables 4.5 and 4.6 describe the reasons for excluding studies. Most studies were excluded at the first stage because they were not studies about spelling or because they were not trials. It is quite usual to exclude a large percentage of studies at the first stage because they are outside the scope of the review. Most studies were excluded at the second stage of screening because they were not randomized controlled trials.

All of the papers in the 'map' were randomized controlled trials. However, for the in-depth review only RCTs evaluating interventions to improve spelling in 'normally achieving' children aged 7–14 were included. The remaining eleven papers in the in-depth review fulfilled these criteria.

Data extraction

Once screening has been completed and potentially relevant studies identified, the relevant data for the review are extracted onto a standardized data extraction form. Box 4.2 gives an outline of a minimum data extraction sheet that can be used to extract the key data from randomized trials.

Box 4.2 Example of data extraction sheet

Author:	
Year:	
Country:	Country where the research was carried out.
Publication type:	Journal article; book chapter; unpublished dissertation; report.
Reference:	Full reference including title of journal, volume, page numbers.
Source:	Where the reference was identified (e.g., PsycINFO, hand search).
Setting:	Setting where study was carried out (e.g., elementary school).
Objective:	Objective of the study as stated by the authors.

Outcome measures:	All outcome measures as stated by the authors in the methods section.
Design:	Type of RCT (e.g., cluster or individual or cross-over).
Participants:	Detailed description of participants involved in study (e.g., age, gender, ethnicity, socio-economic factors, learner characteristics).
Intervention:	Detailed description of the intervention.
Control:	Detailed description of control treatment.
Results (as reported by authors):	All results including those in narrative and in tables.
Effect size (as reported by authors):	If authors report effect size(s) include.
Effect size (as calculated by reviewers):	If authors do not include effect size reviewers need to calculate.
Comments:	Details about study quality (e.g., attrition rate); if the RCT is reported elsewhere give reference.

Data extraction sheets should be piloted on several trials and amended if necessary before extracting data on all the trials. As part of its methodological work in research synthesis the EPPI-Centre has developed detailed data extraction guidelines and tools for use with the DfES-funded EPPI-Centre review groups (see http://eppi.ioe.ac.uk/EPPIWeb/home.aspx). It has been suggested that data extraction should be undertaken by the reviewer 'blind' to the article's authors and the journal to reduce the risk of bias (Egger and Davey-Smith 2001). The reasoning behind this is that reviewers might be more favourable in their judgement towards a paper that they know has been published in a prestigious journal or has originated from a highly respected research group. However, masking reviewers to the identity of papers is extremely time-consuming as all papers need to be photocopied with the authors and identifying features of the journal removed by an independent person. However, a randomized trial comparing blinded with unblinded data extraction found no significant difference in results between the approaches (Berlin 1997).

Box 4.3 is an example of a completed data extraction sheet from a systematic review of randomized controlled trials evaluating interventions in adult literacy and numeracy (Torgerson, Porthouse, Brooks 2003). Data were extracted using the data extraction sheet in Box 4.2. The paper was double data extracted by two reviewers who then discussed the data extraction and resolved any differences. The sheet summarizes the key aspects of the trial, for example bibliographic details and information about the aims of the study, the intervention and the outcomes measured, characteristics of the participants and a summary of the results of the trial.

Box 4.3 Example of completed data extraction sheet

Author:	Batchelder and Rachal
Year:	2000
Country:	USA
Publication type:	Journal article
Setting:	Maximum security prison
Objective:	To examine the efficacy of using computer-assisted instruction (CAI) with inmates participating in a prison education programme compared with inmates participating in a traditional instruction programme using an experimental design.
Study topic:	Literacy and numeracy CAI Incarcerated population
Outcome measures:	Comprehensive Adult Student Assessment System (CASAS) maths and reading post-tests.

Design:	RCT (individual), digit table.
Participants:	n = 75 male inmates in maximum security prison. Two ethnic groups: African-American inmates (n = 56) and Caucasians (n = 15).
Intervention: I:	Participants received GED instructional material for 1 hour per day on computers for a total of 80 hours over a 4-week period in mathematics or language. Also traditional instruction for 3 hours per day in English, maths, history and science.
Control:	Participants received traditional instruction in English, maths, history and science for 4 hours per day for a total of 80 hours over a 4-week period.
Results: (as reported by authors):	Achievement scores of inmates in the intervention group were not significantly higher than those in the control group.

Group	Mean	SD	n
CASAS maths post-test			
Group 1: Experimental	221.9	12.3	36
Group 2: Control	217.0	17.9	35
CASAS reading post-test			
Group 1: Experimental	227.4	13.5	36
Group 2: Control	223.4	17.5	35

Effect size:	CASAS maths: No significant difference Unadjusted effect size = 0.16 CASA reading: No significant difference Unadjusted effect size = 0.26
Effect size (as calculated by reviewers):	No difference between I and C
Comments:	Study also reported as: Batchelder 2000 Attrition: n = 4

A key issue with respect to data extraction is the reviewer decision about whether a study is actually a randomized trial or not. Slavin (1986) has noted that some meta-analyses of 'randomized controlled trials' in education included non-randomized controlled trials. The reviewers were unclear of the difference. In a randomized controlled trial participants are *randomly assigned* to their instructional group (intervention or control). Unfortunately, randomization as a procedure for allocating individuals or clusters to an intervention or control group is not always well understood by educational researchers (Fitz-Gibbon 2000) and often not clearly described.

Phrases that are often used to describe random allocation in educational trials include:

> 'Children were paired on the basis of gender and age and allocated *randomly* using random number tables or coin toss to the treatment'
>
> 'Using random number tables or coin toss children were assigned to their groups'
>
> 'Using restricted or stratified or blocked allocation schedule participants were assigned to their groups'
>
> 'Intact classrooms or schools were matched on class size and a member of each pair was randomly assigned to the intervention'

In contrast the following do *not* describe random allocation:

> 'We took a random sample of children from schools that were not implementing the curriculum and compared them with a random sample of children in the intervention schools'
>
> 'After the schools/children/students had been randomly assigned we asked teachers to identify, for post-test, those children who they felt had benefited most from the intervention'

> 'Two schools were chosen to take part and one school was randomly allocated to receive the new curriculum'

The last statement may appear to be a 'cluster randomized trial' but it is not. Randomizing schools is a perfectly legitimate method of performing a randomized controlled trial; however, if there is only one cluster in each arm of the trial this cannot control for school effects, whether random allocation was used or not. It is recommended that two-armed cluster trials should have at least eight clusters (i.e. four in each arm) and preferably more to allow randomization to balance out any school level confounders (Ukoumunne *et al.* 1998).

Even knowing whether to describe a trial as being randomized or not can sometimes be difficult to ascertain. For example, it is not clear from the published report of a trial evaluating phonological awareness training by Hatcher and colleagues (1994) whether or not it is a randomized controlled trial. Therefore, if one relied solely on the published report such a study would probably be classified as a controlled study, not the more rigorous randomized trial. However, the children in that study were actually allocated to their treatment groups in a randomized fashion (Hatcher, personal communication, 2001). In some reviews, therefore, it may be necessary to contact the authors for more details about their studies to facilitate both data extraction and quality appraisal.

Sometimes studies claim to have produced matched pairs of children or students and then randomly allocated one member of a pair to the intervention. This process should produce exactly equal numbers in each group. The presence of uneven numbers in intervention and control groups when using a matched-pair design gives cause for concern about the quality of the study. In contrast, when small studies use simple allocation it is perfectly possible to have exactly equal numbers but this is unlikely. Nevertheless many small studies using 'simple' randomization or random number tables have suspiciously good numerical equivalence. Numerical balance, in small trials, is only likely if some form of stratified allocation mechanism is used. In contrast, large trials, whilst unlikely to have exact numerical balance, should have an approximate 50:50 split. An interesting example of inconsistent allocation occurred in a study of an adult education programme in six counties in California. Altogether 20,000 participants were randomized (by simple allocation methods). There were approximately equal numbers of participants in only one county; in the remaining five counties the percentage allocated to the experimental group ranged from 68 per cent to 86 per cent (Martinson and Friedlander 1994, cited in Torgerson, Porthouse, Brooks 2003). This disparity in group-size was never satisfactorily explained.

Summary

- The protocol is an *a priori* statement of the research question, aims and methods of the review. It includes the procedures for searching and screening, data extraction, quality appraisal and synthesis.
- The literature search should focus on the electronic databases, but may include other methods of retrieval, for example hand searching of key journals, searching bibliographies of other reviews, personal contacts.
- Ideally, screening, data extraction and quality appraisal should be undertaken by two researchers, working independently.

5

Quality Appraisal

The main reason for undertaking a randomized controlled trial is to obtain evidence with a high degree of internal validity. Although RCTs are widely regarded as the 'gold standard' of effectiveness research, clearly their results are more reliable when the trials are of high quality. Over the last decade trial methodologists working in the health field have developed a set of guidelines that trialists should adhere to if they wish to report a good-quality trial – these have been published as the Consolidated Standards for Reporting Trials (CONSORT statement) (Altman 1996). The motivation for CONSORT was the poor quality of so many of the RCTs that have been published in the health care field, which may misinform policy. Many major medical journals now insist that reports of RCTs conform to the CONSORT guidelines (Altman 1996).

Low-quality trials have also been undertaken and published in the field of educational research. In a systematic review of the effects of information and communication technology (ICT) on the teaching and learning of spelling it was noted that the quality of trials included in that review was generally low (Torgerson and Elbourne 2002). At present in the field of educational research there is no equivalent of the CONSORT statement. However, educational researchers have long recognized the need to 'quality-appraise' RCTs in education (Slavin 1986, Troia 1999, Torgerson and Elbourne 2002).

The issue of trial quality has increased in importance in

the field of health care research. Methodological reviews have described a relatively high prevalence of poor-quality trials, which can mislead health care practice and policy (Schulz *et al.* 1995, Kjaergard *et al.* 2001). Indeed, recently a large methodological analysis sought to explain the puzzling phenomenon of larger trials yielding smaller effect sizes, on average, than smaller trials, even when they are attempting to address the same question. Kjaergard and colleagues (2001) examined the quality of large and small trials and found that large trials tended to be of better quality than small studies. After they had taken quality of trial methodology into account the difference in observed effect sizes between large and small studies disappeared. This indicates, therefore, that poor-quality studies, rather than small trials, could be a source of bias when included in a meta-analysis. This problem is likely to affect educational trials as well as health care studies. For example, Lipsey and Wilson (1993) noted that educational and psychological trials with sample sizes of more than 100 yielded smaller average effect sizes compared with smaller trials. More recently, in a systematic review of phonemic awareness training Ehri, Nunes, Stahl, Willows (2001) found effect size was inversely related to sample size in reading and spelling outcomes. It is possible that size may be a marker for poor trial quality in education just as it is in health care.

Educational researchers are aware of the potential problems of poor-quality trials and many have produced sets of quality criteria in order to classify studies as being rigorous or not. For example the EPPI-Centre has developed detailed guidelines and tools for quality appraisal of randomized controlled trials and all other study types. Table 5.1 contains an example of quality criteria that were developed to assess the quality of controlled trials in phonological awareness training (Troia 1999). As well as listing the various criteria, often a 'scoring' system is used so that a summary score can be given to a trial.

Table 5.1 Troia's study quality criteria relating to internal validity

Validity criteria	Weighting
Random assignment	3
Control group received alternative intervention to control for Hawthorne effect	3
Exposure to similar materials for control group	1
Counterbalancing of teachers	2
Treatment explicitly described	2
Criterion-based intervention	1
Equivalent instructional time	3
Equivalent mortality rates	1

Measurement of study quality, however, is not necessarily an objective exercise. The use of any quality score can be fraught with difficulty. For example, Juni and colleagues quality appraised seventeen health care trials, from a meta-analysis, with 25 different quality scales (Juni *et al.* 1999). They found that, for twelve scales, the effect sizes were the same when trials were rated as high or low quality. However, for six scales, high-quality trials showed little or no benefit of treatment compared with low-quality studies, whilst the remaining seven scales showed the opposite. Thus, quality assurance scales can give very different results depending on the items included and the weights given to individual items.

If quality criteria use a system of 'weighting' or 'adding up' there is a risk of classifying a trial as being of 'good' quality simply because it performs well on many of the criteria. However, if the trial has a fatal flaw in one of the most important aspects of trial design, the results of the trial may be unreliable. On some scales studies can score highly if they are well reported rather than well conducted (Juni *et al.*

2001). Juni and colleagues (2001) explain how a trial can be defined as being of 'high' quality on one widely used scale in assessing the quality of health care trials even if the authors report that they did *not* use random allocation because the scale emphasizes reporting rather than actual performance.

Many aspects of study or trial design can affect the outcome of a study. The most important design criteria relate to its internal validity. If a study is not internally valid, then the observed effect sizes from a study may be incorrect. Clearly the study design with the greatest internal validity is the experimental method using randomization to assemble comparable groups (Cook and Campbell 1979). Despite randomization, however, forms of selection bias can be introduced during the trial (see Torgerson, and Torgerson, 2003b for a full discussion). If researchers subvert the allocation schedule this can introduce a source of bias. This phenomenon has been documented both in health care trials (Schulz *et al.* 1995) and criminal justice studies (Boruch 1997). Ideally, trial allocation should be undertaken by an independent person, as this will reduce the risk of the allocation being subverted. A symptom of a problem with randomization is if the 'baseline' variables differ between the groups (i.e. there is baseline imbalance).

Once randomization has occurred bias can still be introduced if outcomes are not measured blindly at post-test. If the researchers or assessors are aware of the allocated group they may, consciously or unconsciously, give higher marks to those students in one group. Outcome assessment should be undertaken by someone who is 'masked' or 'blinded' to group assignment (Cook and Campbell 1979).

Two other important aspects of trial design include attrition and intention to teach. Attrition, often referred to as 'mortality' in educational papers (Troia 1999), is when participants drop out of the study between randomization and post-test. If the drop-out rate is either high or unequal between the groups then this can introduce selection bias.

Those who drop out from one group may be different from those who remain in the comparison group. Another analytical problem occurs when not all participants are included in the final analysis. Some researchers undertake 'active treatment' analysis, that is only analysing participants if they receive the intervention to which they were allocated. The most rigorous way to analyse the data is to undertake 'intention to teach' analysis. This is where all participants are analysed in the groups into which they were originally allocated. This may be difficult to achieve in practice as some participants usually 'drop out' and therefore they cannot be included in post-tests.

In summary, to ensure a robust and valid trial one should look for concealed randomization; similar attrition rates; no baseline imbalance; blinded or masked follow-up. Table 5.2 contains a modified version of the CONSORT criteria, widely used in health care, which can be used to describe the quality of trials identified in education.

The most important aspects of quality relate to the internal validity of the trial and these are highlighted in italics in Table 5.2. There are, however, other important aspects of trial quality that are included in the CONSORT quality check. Three of these relate to the issue of sample size or the possibility of a Type II error. A Type II error occurs when there is a 'true' difference between groups, but the sample size is insufficient to demonstrate this difference as being statistically significant. The larger the study, the less likely it is to suffer a Type II error.

Sample size

In the field of education, as in health care, most effective experimental innovations yield small to moderate positive effects (Kulik and Kulik 1989, Lipsey and Wilson 1993). Therefore, researchers seeking statistical significance must

Table 5.2 Modified CONSORT quality criteria

Was the study population adequately described? (i.e. were the important characteristics of the randomized participants described, e.g. age, gender?)
Was the minimum important difference described? (i.e. was the smallest educationally important effect size described?)
Was the target sample size adequately determined?
Was intention to treat analysis used? (i.e. were all participants who were randomized included in the follow-up and analysis?)
Was the unit of randomization described (i.e. individual participants or groups of participants)?
Were the participants allocated using random number tables, coin flip, computer generation?
Was the randomization process concealed from the investigators? (i.e. were the researchers who were recruiting participants to the trial blind to the participant's allocation until after that participant had been included in the trial?)
Were follow-up measures administered blind? (i.e. were the researchers who administered the outcome measures blind to treatment allocation?)
Was estimated effect on primary and secondary outcome measures stated?
Was precision of effect size estimated (confidence intervals)?
Were summary data presented in sufficient detail to permit alternative analyses or replication?
Was the discussion of the study findings consistent with the data?

use large sample sizes. The probability of an 'educationally significant' difference being also statistically significant is partly a function of sample size. Small sample sizes can miss important differences between the treatment groups. Importantly for systematic reviewers, small sample sizes often lead to null or non-significant *negative* results, which can lead to the study not being published. Such trials will be excluded from any review and only positive, statistically significant, trials will be included. This will lead to an over-optimistic assessment of the benefit of a given intervention.

In order to ascertain whether or not a study is large enough, an educationally significant difference needs to be calculated. In their review of educational and psychological experiments, Lipsey and Wilson (1993) found that for effective interventions the effect sizes ranged, on average, from about 0.25 to 0.50. If it is assumed that, as a minimum, a trial ought to be large enough to detect at least half an effect size then, statistically it can be demonstrated that to have an 80 per cent chance of detecting half a standard deviation difference between two groups with a significance level of 5 per cent, a trial requires 63 children in each group (i.e. 126 in total). Trials smaller than this run a high risk of missing an important difference in outcome between the experimental and control groups. Indeed, even a sample size of several hundred would be too small to detect the benefit observed in the Tennessee experiment of class sizes. To observe the modest benefit of smaller class sizes would require several thousand children. Whether this small benefit is educationally 'significant' or 'worthwhile' is a matter for teachers, parents and policy-makers to debate.

Confidence intervals

The point estimate of an effect from any trial is bounded by uncertainty. For instance, a large effect can be statistically insignificant because the sample size is too small. One way of representing the boundaries of uncertainty around an estimate of effect is to use confidence intervals (usually 95%). The confidence interval represents (given the constraints of the sample size) where 95 per cent of the results would lie, if the experiment were repeated 100 times. Confidence intervals are important because they show the uncertainty that surrounds the point estimate of effect. For example, Weiner (1994) showed an effect of phonemic awareness training that was not statistically significant with an effect size of about 0.3 among 30 pupils, which is considered a reasonable effect size in educational research. The upper confidence limit included an even larger effect size of about 1.0, indicating that the trial was too small to exclude a very large difference in effect. There was a real danger, therefore, that this trial experienced a Type II error: that is erroneously concluding there was no effect when in fact there was one.

In Table 5.3 the CONSORT quality criteria are applied to a sample of RCTs from a systematic review of interventions in adult education. This table is fairly representative of the reporting quality of educational trials. No trial report, for example, outlines the reasoning behind sample size calculation or reports confidence intervals. For internal validity criteria no trial reports whether the randomization process was undertaken independently and few trials report blinded outcome assessment and intention to teach analysis.

Note in this table (Table 5.3) for quality assurance, quality criteria are not given a weight or simply added up. It may be advisable for the reviewer to make a judgement relating to individual trials as to whether a given quality criterion that has not been fulfilled represents a 'fatal flaw' and undermines that study's results. In other words, undertaking a systematic review is not a mechanistic exercise: it requires skill and experience to interpret the results.

Summary

- The most important aspects of trial design relate to internal validity. If a RCT is not internally valid, the observed effect sizes may be incorrect.
- The quality of randomized trials included in systematic reviews should be assessed on their internal validity.
- Various sets of quality criteria to appraise RCTs have been developed.

Table 5.3 Example of the 'CONSORT' quality checklist applied to RCTs

	Batchelder and Rachal 2000	Bean and Wilson 1989	Cheek and Lindsey 1994	Martinson and Friedlander 1994	McKane and Greene 1996	Nicol and Anderson 2000	Rich and Shepherd 1993	Shrum 1985	St Pierre *et al.* 1993
Was the study population adequately described? (i.e. were the important characteristics of the randomized adults described, e.g. age, gender?)	Y	Y	Y	N	N	Y	Y	Y	N
Was the minimum important difference described? (i.e. was the smallest educationally important effect size described?)	N/S	N/S	N/S	N/S	N/S	N/S	N/S	N/S	N/S
Was the target sample size adequately determined?	N/S	N/S	N/S	N/S	N/S	N/S	N/S	N/S	N/S
Was intention to treat analysis used? (i.e. were all adults who were randomized included in the follow-up and analysis?)	N	N	N	N	N	N/S	Y	N/S	N

	Batchelder and Rachal 2000	Bean and Wilson 1989	Cheek and Lindsey 1994	Martinson and Friedlander 1994	McKane and Greene 1996	Nicol and Anderson 2000	Rich and Shepherd 1993	Shrum 1985	St Pierre *et al.* 1993
Was the unit of randomization described (i.e. individual adults or groups of adults)?	Y ind	Y Ind	Y ind	Y Ind	Y ind	Y ind	Y ind	Y ind	Y ind
Were the participants allocated using random number tables, coin flip, computer generation?	Y	N/S	N/S	N/S	N/S	N/S	N/S	Y	N/S
Was the randomization process concealed from the investigators? (i.e. were the researchers who were recruiting adults to the trial blind to the adult's allocation until after that adult had been included in the trial?)	N/S	N/S	N/S	N/S	N/S	N/S	N/S	N/S	U
Were follow-up measures administered blind? (i.e. were the researchers who administered the outcome measures blind to treatment allocation?)	N/S	N/S	N/S	N/S	N/S	N/S	Y	N/S	Y
Was estimated effect on primary and secondary outcome measures stated?	Y	Y	Y	U	Y	Y	Y	Y	Y

	Batchelder and Rachal 2000	Bean and Wilson 1989	Cheek and Lindsey 1994	Martinson and Friedlander 1994	McKane and Greene 1996	Nicol and Anderson 2000	Rich and Shepherd 1993	Shrum 1985	St Pierre *et al.* 1993
Was precision of effect size estimated (confidence intervals)?	N/S	N	N	N/S	N/S	N	N/S	N/S	N
Were summary data presented in sufficient detail to permit alternative analyses or replication?	Y	Y	Y	U	Y	Y	Y	N	Y
Was the discussion of the study findings consistent with the data?	Y	N	Y	N	Y	N	Y	Y	Y

N/S = not stated; U = unclear

Source: Torgerson *et al.* (2003) 'A systematic review and meta-analysis of randomised controlled trials evaluating interventions in adult literacy and numeracy', *Journal of Research in Reading*, 26 (3), 2003.

6

Publication Bias

A systematic review of randomized controlled trials provides an unbiased estimate of the effect of an intervention if one of two conditions is fulfilled: firstly, if *all* the relevant trials are included in the review; or, secondly, if a random *sample* of all the trials ever undertaken is included in the review. In many reviews it is unlikely that the first condition will be fulfilled. If the literature is particularly large then it is likely that some trials will be overlooked. As long as the trials that are missed do not depart in any significant or systematic way from the trials that are included, then the estimate of the intervention effect will not be biased. In a meta-analysis, a statistically non-significant estimate of effect could be due to missing trials. This is because the greater the number of trials included in the meta-analysis the more precise will be the estimate of effect. Trials 'missing at random' will not, on average, alter the direction of the effect size, but their non-inclusion will reduce precision.

A more serious problem occurs, however, when trials that are not included in the review are missing because they are unpublished, and have characteristics that make them different from published studies. Unpublished studies tend to demonstrate negative or null effects. Therefore, a systematic review will tend to retrieve a sample of trials that are positive, which will give an inflated estimate of any effect of the intervention. If the search strategy for a systematic review includes searching bibliographies of non-systematic reviews these will tend to cite the positive trials more often than the negative studies. It is perfectly possible, therefore, by excluding trials 'not missing at random' to either overestimate the effectiveness of an intervention or, more seriously, to reverse the direction of effect. This may result in a review concluding that a harmful intervention is actually beneficial.

Historically, some journals have not published trials that do not produce 'significant' or different findings. Some journal editors and referees, therefore, will reject as being 'uninteresting' a trial that reports no difference between an intervention and control group. Rejection of a paper by journals and referees may be accompanied by a 'scientific rationale' justifying the refusal to publish. For example, consider two small trials both containing 30 participants. One trial shows a large positive effect size of 0.75, which is statistically significant, whilst the other shows an effect size of 0.30, which is not significant. The first trial might be accepted for publication on the basis that it has shown a large and potentially relevant benefit, whilst the other might be rejected because its sample size is too small. Because both trials have tiny sample sizes their point estimate of effect is likely to be in error. Let us assume the 'true' effect lies somewhere in between: this can be estimated through using a meta-analysis. If we combine these two small trials in a meta-analysis we can show that the 'average' effect size is 0.50, but this effect is not quite statistically significant (95% confidence interval = -0.01 to 1.02, $p = 0.055$). Therefore, the trial that was accepted for publication 'overestimates' the true effect, whilst the second trial that underestimates the true effect remains unpublished. On the basis of the two trials we might, therefore, call for another large and well-conducted study to confirm the suggestion of a benefit.

If publication bias were particularly severe we might identify a dozen small trials all producing 'over-estimated' effect sizes. Performing a meta-analysis of these might lead us to conclude that the large benefit justifies the cost of implementing the intervention, whereas the actual effect of the intervention could be so small as not to justify implementation.

Because publication bias can produce misleading results it is important that its presence is detected and discussed in the review. One relatively simple way of looking for publication bias is through the use of a 'funnel plot'.

Funnel plot

A funnel plot graphically displays the effect sizes from identified trials along with some estimate of their sampling error (e.g. sample size). All trials only produce an *estimate* of the effect of the intervention, which is bounded by uncertainty. The effect of chance underpins the design and interpretation of trials. A small trial can produce some surprisingly good or poor results, merely by chance. The larger the trial the less likely is the effect of chance on the outcome. Combining small trials that have positive and negative findings has a similar effect to undertaking a single large trial, and these chance effects for positive and negative findings will balance each other out.

We can use the increased variability of small trials compared with large trials to establish whether or not there is evidence for publication bias. As the larger trials produce effect sizes closest to the 'true' value compared with small trials we can show the relationship between size and effect in a funnel plot. In a funnel plot the effect size of a trial is plotted on the x-axis against its sample size on the y. The smaller and less precise trials will be scattered along the x-axis whilst the larger and more precise studies will be clustered together. Where there is no publication bias the trials will form an inverted funnel shape, hence, the term 'funnel plot'. In Figure 6.1 a hypothetical funnel plot is shown where there is no evidence of publication bias.

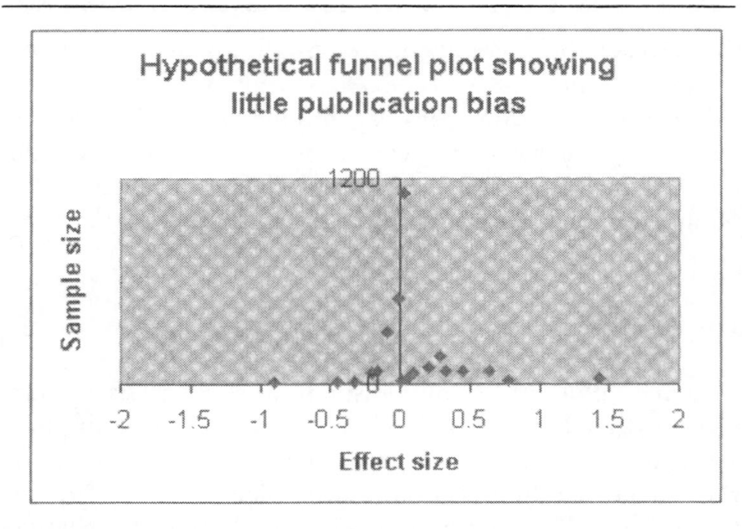

Figure 6.1 Funnel plot showing no evidence for publication bias

The figure shows a hypothetical review of a subject area where there is little evidence for any difference between the groups in terms of an overall benefit. Note how the small trials show a large variation in effect with some showing a large positive effect size of 1 or more but with others showing a similarly large negative effect size. If all of these trials were combined in a meta-analysis it is likely that it would show no overall effect.

In contrast, Figure 6.2 shows a funnel plot, taken from a recent systematic review, where there is evidence of publication bias (Torgerson, Porthouse, Brooks 2003). Note that all the trials, including the very small ones, demonstrate a positive effect. It is very unlikely, given the tiny sample sizes, that all eight trials would, by chance, have shown a positive and mostly quite large effect size. Therefore, it is likely that there are other trials that have either not been published or are only available as obscure reports, and which were not identified by the search strategy. These other trials would have either negative or null effects.

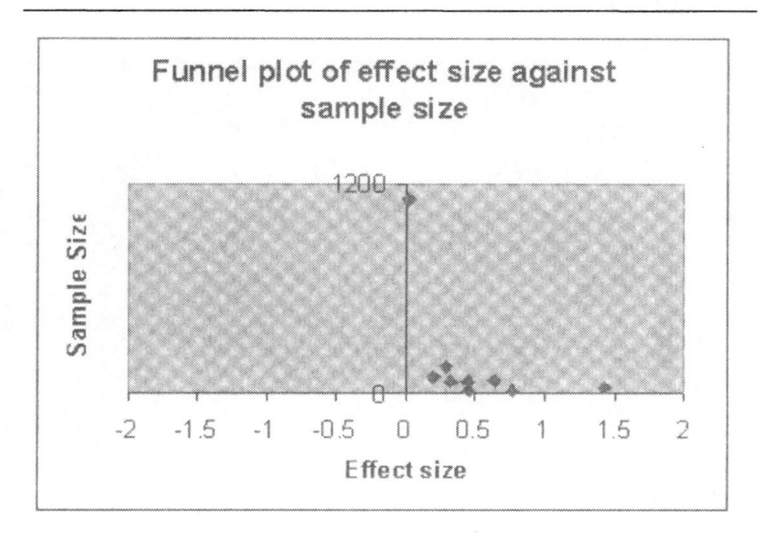

Figure 6.2 Funnel plot of RCTs in adult literacy showing publication bias

In Figure 6.3 another funnel plot shows evidence of publication bias. The data to construct the plot were taken from a systematic review by Ehri, Nunes, Willows and colleagues (2001). In the Ehri review of systematic phonics instruction interventions, one of the inclusion criteria was journal articles that had been peer-refereed. Including this criterion will potentially increase the risk of overestimating the effect size of the intervention, as it is more likely that negative studies will have been excluded. As Figure 6.3 shows, there were no studies reporting a negative effect of systematic phonics instruction compared with all forms of control despite the small sample sizes of the included studies.

Therefore, any results of a meta-analysis from trials present in the funnel plot should be treated with a high degree of caution, as they are likely to overestimate the effectiveness of the interventions.

A problem with funnel plots is that they become more unreliable at detecting the existence of publication bias in

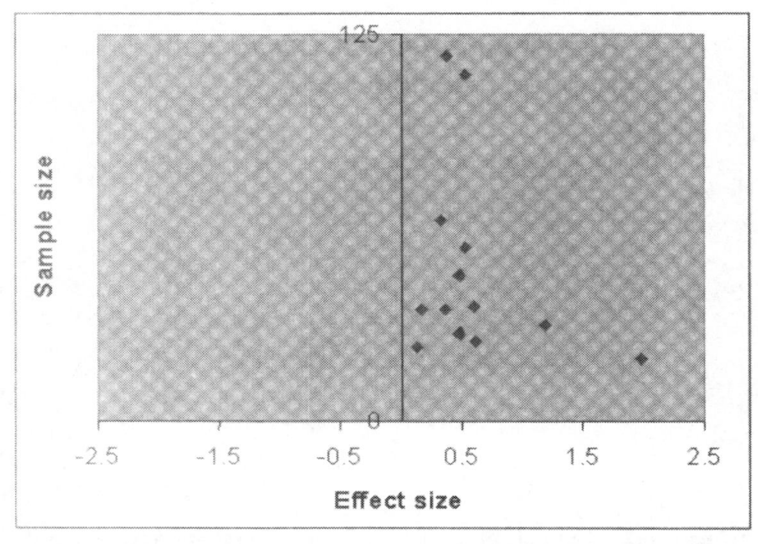

Figure 6.3 Funnel plot of randomized trials from a systematic review of systematic phonics instruction showing presence of publication bias

the presence of very few trials. For example, if in the review of studies in Figure 6.2 the two largest trials had not been undertaken or had been missed on the search strategy, the funnel plot would indicate little publication bias.

Another way of examining publication bias is to compare the effect sizes of reports published in peer review journals with those in unpublished reports or theses. Because authors, referees and journal editors are less likely to write up and publish negative trials, it is likely that trials that have been written up as a report to the funding body of the research or as a thesis for the requirements of a degree will demonstrate different effect sizes, if publication bias exists. Again, in the field of adult literacy education this appears to be the case. When the mean effect sizes of the studies that have been published (that is, formally, for example in refereed journals) are compared with those that are 'unpublished' (that is, published informally, for example as in-house reports or mimeographs, or in the so-called 'grey' literature) we may observe a different estimate. The six published studies show a pooled effect size of 0.49 (95% CI 0.17 to 0.82, $p = 0.003$), whereas the three 'unpublished' studies show a lower effect size of 0.26 (95% CI –0.07 to 0.59, $p = 0.13$). Clearly, the unpublished studies are 'published' in the sense that their reports are obtainable and are in the public domain. Nevertheless, these reports tend to show an effect size approximately half the size of the effect sizes of the studies that are published in journals. Studies that have never been published in any form are likely to have even smaller effect sizes. These data coupled with the funnel plot indicate that there are probably significant numbers of 'missing' studies with either negative, null or very small positive effect sizes. Again this kind of result indicates that the results should be treated cautiously.

If publication bias is detected, what should be done? There are a number of methods for attempting to 'weight' the results of the review to take into account publication bias, none of which is completely satisfactory. One method, 'trim and fill' is basically to remove 'outlying' trials from the funnel plot until we have a symmetrical plot and then reintroduce the trials with a corresponding hypothetical trial with the opposite effect (Sterne *et al.* 2001). This approach, assumes however, that the missing studies have the inverse values of the outlying identified trials, which may not be the case. Another approach is to only undertake a meta-analysis on trials with large sample sizes (e.g. > 100). The reasoning behind this is that usually only small trials tend not to be published and that these missing small trials will all be negative, which may not be a realistic assumption. This approach will, however, negate an important rationale of meta-analysis: combining small studies to yield a more precise estimate of effect (Lipsey and Wilson 2001). Indeed, in the author's meta-analysis of RCTs evaluating the effectiveness of information and communication technology on spelling, this approach would have resulted in the rejection of all of the identified studies (Torgerson and Elbourne 2002).

Sometimes studies are published with missing data. If no effect is found, authors may report that 'there were no significant differences between the groups' but may not report the mean values to allow their inclusion in a meta-analysis. Writing directly to the authors may yield the necessary data in some instances. Published studies with missing data can be included in a meta-analysis with simulated data to show no effect, which may be better than not including them at all (Lipsey and Wilson 2001).

Publication bias is a real threat to the validity of any systematic review. It is important that the reviewer should examine the data for evidence of such bias. It is also important to note that absence of evidence for such bias does not necessarily mean absence of bias. If there seems to be bias this should be highlighted in the discussion of the review and some steps can be taken to examine its influence, such as the use of sensitivity analysis, which is discussed later. It is important that all randomized controlled trials (even small underpowered trials) should be published whatever their results. Given the wide availability of electronic or web-based publishing it will be less likely in the future that articles will disappear without trace in obscure paper journals.

Quality assessment of systematic reviews

Systematic reviews can, clearly, vary in their quality. As with quality assessment of randomized trials, there have been a number of attempts to derive quality assurance scales in order to quality appraise systematic reviews (Shea *et al.* 2001). Recently a quality checklist of systematic reviews – the Quality of Reporting of Meta-Analyses (QUORUM) –

checklist has been developed, which has been compared against a number of other quality assurance scales (Shea *et al.* 2001). It may be helpful before commencing a systematic review to check that the review broadly follows the QUORUM checklist, which seems to be more comprehensive than other quality assurance scales.

Box 6.1 Key features of QUORUM statement (adapted for educational studies)

Introduction:	Explicitly state educational problem and rationale for review.
Methods	
Searching:	State sources of information (e.g., names of databases; hand searching of key journals), search restrictions (e.g., year, publication language, published and or unpublished).
Selection:	Inclusion and exclusion criteria.
Validity assessment:	Quality assessment (e.g., blinded follow-up).
Data abstraction:	Process used (e.g., double data extraction).
Study characteristics:	Type of study design, student characteristics, details of intervention, outcomes, how was educational heterogeneity assessed?
Data synthesis:	How were data combined? Measures of effect, statistical testing and confidence intervals, handling of missing data, sensitivity and subgroup analyses, assessment of publication bias.
Results	
Trial flow:	Provide a profile of trials identified and reasons for inclusion/exclusion.
Study characteristics:	Provide descriptive data for each trial (e.g., age, setting, class size, intervention).
Quantitative data synthesis:	Report agreement between reviewers on selection and validity assessment; present summary results; report data needed to calculate effect sizes and confidence intervals

	(i.e., number; mean; standard deviations by group).
Discussion:	Summarize key findings and educational inferences. Interpret results in light of all the evidence; acknowledge potential biases in review and suggest areas for future research.

Source: Shea *et al.* (2001)

Summary

- Publication bias can occur in a systematic review if studies 'not missing at random' are excluded: this can overestimate the effect or reverse the direction of effect.
- Publication bias can threaten the validity of a systematic review. Therefore it is important that its presence is detected and discussed.
- One relatively simple way of looking for publication bias is through the use of a 'funnel plot'.
- As with quality assessment of randomized trials, there have been a number of attempts to derive quality assurance scales in order to quality appraise systematic reviews.
- Before undertaking a review it may be helpful to check that it broadly follows the QUORUM checklist.

7

Data Synthesis and Meta-analysis

Data from randomized trials can be synthesized in a number of different ways. Firstly, a 'qualitative' overview of the studies can be undertaken. The basic characteristics of the studies are described, including their methodological strengths and weaknesses. This aspect of the review requires a good understanding of the methodology of trial design and execution. Subject specialism is also important when understanding the intervention. For example, a study might compare an intervention delivered through information and communication technology with the same intervention delivered through 'conventional' teaching. However, it is possible that the ICT intervention is quite different from the 'treatment' delivered in the control condition. Therefore, in such circumstances one could not disentangle the effects of ICT from the effects of the different teaching strategies.

Another way of synthesizing the identified studies is through the use of 'vote' counting (see Davies 2000 for a full discussion). For example, if ten trials were identified in a review, this method would state that six showed a positive effect (three of which were statistically significant), three showed a negative effect and one showed no effect. Vote counting may be useful in describing the overall effects of the trials, especially when a meta-analysis is not possible. However, this method should be treated with caution. If, for example, one of the ten trials that showed no effect contained 1000 participants and was a rigorously designed and executed RCT, this study would carry more weight than the nine remaining trials (particularly if they were small and poorly designed and conducted). On the other hand, if all the trials were of similar quality and size, and there was no evidence of publication bias, vote counting may give some indication as to whether or not there could be an overall effect.

Table 7.1 is an example of a summary data synthesis table for a systematic review of the effect of unpaid classroom assistants on children's reading. It presents information about the aims of each RCT, the setting, the participants, the intervention and control 'treatments' and the outcome measurements.

Table 7.2 shows a 'qualitative' synthesis of RCTs identified in a systematic review of the effect of unpaid 'volunteers' on children's reading. Four RCTs indicated a positive effect of the intervention on outcomes, one of which was statistically significant. Three RCTs indicated a negative effect, and one was equivocal. These data suggest no evidence of a benefit of volunteer classroom assistants on reading outcomes. This finding was supported by a meta-analysis of the four most homogeneous trials (see Figure 7.1, p. 84). This indicated a small, pooled effect size of 0.19, which was not statistically significant (95% confidence interval –0.31 to 0.68, $p = 0.54$). The descriptive tables, however, show that one trial was of reasonably high quality and appeared to show consistent positive effects (Baker 2000). For the researcher proposing to undertake another trial in this area, replication of a study similar to Baker's could be worthwhile.

Meta-analysis is a statistical technique of 'pooling' data from two or more randomized trials. The value of a meta-analysis lies in the fact that it reduces the random errors experienced by a single study and can lead to a more precise estimate of the overall effect. There are a number of

Table 7.1 Description of randomized controlled trials

Study reference	Study setting and design	Intervention	Type of volunteer and training	Control	Main outcome measures
Baker *et al*. 2000	USA, individually randomized trial, teachers selected children with below average reading skills from 24 first-grade classrooms. 127 children originally randomized, a third dropped out leaving 84.	Children received 1 hour to 1 hour 30 minutes tutoring two times a week for two years (average 73 sessions, SD 10.9).	Middle-aged volunteers (gender not stated) recruited mainly from the business community given 1–2 hours of training.	Normal classroom instruction.	Woodcock Reading Mastery Test–Revised (Word Identification subtest), Oral Reading Fluency, Word and Passage Comprehension.
Elliott *et* al. 2000	UK, cluster randomized trial of intact classes from primary schools in poor socio-economical areas in north-east of England. Two parallel reception classes from each of three primary schools randomized. 140 children at start of trial, 41 dropped out.	Volunteers worked with children alongside classroom teacher all the time except for practical lessons (e.g. physical education).	Mainly mature women.	Children in control classes received normal classroom lessons from teacher.	Wechsler Objective Reading Development Scales (WORD).

Study reference	Study setting and design	Intervention	Type of volunteer and training	Control	Main outcome measures
Loenen 1989	UK, children needing help identified by staff in 16 primary schools in inner London. Children were generally poor readers. 81 were randomized and 81 completed reading comprehension and accuracy post-tests.	Two out of class 30 minute 1 to 1 sessions a week over two terms.	34 volunteers over 35 years, 28 were women, all but one were experienced volunteers. Trained with 3 × 1/5 hour sessions mainly in reading for meaning techniques.	Normal classroom teaching.	Salford Sentence Reading Test (SSRT), Primary Reading Test (PRT).
Morris 1990	USA, second- and third-grade children with low reading ability from schools in low socio-economic areas. 60 children randomized no attrition.	Children given 1 hour tutoring two times a week from 3 p.m. to 4 p.m., 50 hours over a year.	Mixed age, ranging from college students to retired people.	Normal school lessons.	Word recognition, spelling, reading aloud from passages.

Study reference	Study setting and design	Intervention	Type of volunteer and training	Control	Main outcome measures
Rimm-Kaufman 1999	USA, first-grade children (5.5 to 7 years), teachers identified children needing help in literacy. Children paired and individually randomized. 42 children randomized, no attrition.	Three times a week for 45 minutes 1 to 1 tutoring from October to May. Used phonics and reading for meaning.	Well-trained volunteers all over 60 years, half retired teachers, received extensive training for five sessions before start, two bi-monthly sessions during study.	Normal classroom (teachers unaware of who were the control children).	Letters, words, print concepts, writing, dictation and reading level.
Weiss 1988	USA, 'mildly handicapped' students from grades 3 to 6 selected by teachers as those who would benefit most from additional tuition. 17 randomized, 1 lost from control group.	1 to 1 tuition for 20–30 minutes a day for four days a week over 11 weeks with a minimum of 36 sessions (maximum 44).	12 volunteers (8 senior citizens, 9 females, 4 ex-teachers). 5 hour 1 day training plus a follow-up session three weeks later. Trained in paired reading techniques, flash cards, cloze procedure.	Normal classroom teaching.	BASIS, Basic Achievement Skills Individual Screener, Curriculum Based Measurement (Holt reading series).

Study reference	Study setting and design	Intervention	Type of volunteer and training	Control	Main outcome measures
Lee 1980	USA, third- to sixth-grade pupils from either low income groups or from minority groups, children matched in pairs and then randomized. 70 randomized, no attrition.	Pupils tutored as an after-school activity in small groups, 2 to 1 for about 2 hours two times a week.	20 college students (15 women). Undertook seven training modules over 8 weeks.	Normal classroom teaching.	Reading grade equivalent scores.

Source: Torgerson *et al.* (2002) 'Do volunteers in schools help children learn to read? A systematic review of randomised controlled trials', *Educational Studies*, 28(4), 2002.

Table 7.2 Summary of results of randomized controlled trials

Study reference	Mean effect on reading outcome measures		Standardized Difference (95% confidence interval)	Favours volunteers
	Intervention (sample size)	Control (sample size)		
Baker *et al.*				
First Grade	(n=43)	(n=41)		
Word Identification	409.2 (29.7)	398.9 (24.4)	0.38 (−0.05 to 0.81)	Y*
Oral Reading	27.8 (22.8)	18.7 (17.3)	0.45 (0.01 to 0.88)	Y
Passage Comprehension	449.3 (24.4)	443.2 (14.2)	0.30 (−0.13 to 0.73)	Y*
Second Grade				
Word Identification	449.4 (30.2)	437.9 (25.9)	0.41 (−0.03 to 0.84)	Y*
Oral Reading 1	71.3 (35.2)	55.9 (32.1)	0.36 (−0.07 to 0.79)	Y*
Oral Reading 2	61.5 (35.5)	45.9 (29.5)	0.48 (0.04 to 0.91)	Y
Word Comprehension	472.3 (17.3)	465.4 (16.2)	0.41 (−0.02 to 0.84)	Y*
Passage Comprehension	468.9 (16.0)	464.7 (13.1)	0.27 (−0.16 to 0.70)	Y*
Elliott *et al.*	(n=50)	(n=49)		
Reading Accuracy	89.8 (15.6)	90.6 (16.4)	−0.05 (−0.44 to 0.34)	N*
Reading Comprehension	88.5 (14.7)	89.6 (13.8)	−0.08 (−0.47 to 0.32)	N*
Spelling	91.7 (14.3)	93.5 (11.7)	−0.14 (−0.53 to 0.26)	N*
Composite Score	87.9 (17.0)	89.4 (15.4)	−0.09 (−0.49 to 0.30)	N*

Study reference	Mean effect on reading outcome measures		Standardized Difference (95% confidence interval)	Favours volunteers
	Intervention (sample size)	Control (sample size)		
Loenen	(n = 43)	(n = 38)		
Reading Comprehension	19.51 (7.68)	22.31 (7.83)	−0.36 (−0.80 to 0.08)	N*
Reading Accuracy	92.58 (10.78)	97.37 (14.247)	−0.38 (−0.82 to 0.06)	N*
Lee +	(n = 20)	(n = 20)		
Reading Grade Score Change	0.9675 (0.587)	0.9300 (0.759)	0.06 (-0.57 to 0.67)	Y*
Morris	(n = 30)	(n = 30)		
Time Word recognition	58.3 (17.4)	49.9 (19.4)	0.46 (−0.06 to 0.97)	Y*
Untimed Word recognition	77.6 (19.1)	69.8 (22.6)	0.37 (−0.14 to 0.88)	Y*
Basal Word recognition	21.3 (5.2)	18.0 (6.5)	0.56 (0.04 to 1.07)	Y
Passage Comprehension	15.3 (9.4)	9.9 (5.8)	0.69 (0.17 to 1.21)	Y
Spelling (score)	7.7 (4.2)	5.8 (4.3)	0.45 (-0.07 to 0.96)	Y*
Spelling qualitative	85.1 (18.0)	75.4 (21.1)	0.49 (-0.02 to 1.01)	Y*

Study reference	Mean effect on reading outcome measures		Standardized Difference (95% confidence interval)	Favours volunteers
	Intervention (sample size)	Control (sample size)		
Rimm-Kaufman	(n=21)	(n=21)		
Letters	52.86 (1.28)	51.62 (2.80)	0.57 (−0.05 to 1.18)	Y*
Words	13.14 (6.10)	13.38(5.64)	−0.04 (−0.65 to 0.56)	N*
Print Concepts	14.29 (3.18)	14.19 (2.82)	0.03 (−0.57 to 0.64)	N*
Writing	23.05 (11.02)	23.19 (11.40)	−0.01 (−0.62 to 0.59)	N*
Dictation	28.14 (8.43)	26.62 (8.13)	0.18 (−0.42 to 0.79)	Y*
Reading Level	5.86 (3.76)	4.43 (2.82)	0.43 (−0.18 to 1.04)	Y*
Weiss	(n=9)	(n=7)		
BASIS	41.9 (10.1)	43.2 (10.5)	−0.13 (−1.11 to 0.86)	N*
CBM	93.2 (35.2)	106.8 (56.5)	−0.30 (−1.29 to 0.70)	N*

+ Data analysed by tutor to account for clustered nature of data

* Not statistically significant

commercially available software packages that can perform a meta-analysis.

Before a meta-analysis is undertaken a decision needs to be made about whether or not the trials are educationally homogeneous. Lack of homogeneity can sometimes be obvious, such as differences between trials in adult versus child learners. Other sources of 'heterogeneity' may be less obvious, except to the content specialist. Some interventions, whilst appearing to be superficially similar, may have completely different psychological underpinnings and delivery mechanisms. If heterogeneous trials are pooled then the resulting point estimate will not apply to any of the interventions. In the meta-analysis that was undertaken of randomized trials evaluating volunteers, homogeneity was assessed in two ways: the amount of volunteer training, and learner characteristics of the participants. Two trials, therefore, were excluded from the meta-analysis: one because it used volunteers with little training, and the other because it included children who experienced learning disabilities. The reasoning behind such exclusions were as follows. Volunteering is likely to be most effective if volunteers receive training. Including a trial in a meta-analysis of 'untrained' volunteers is likely to dilute any intervention effect and introduce a source of heterogeneity. Similarly, volunteering may have different effects in relation to whether or not the children experience disabilities in learning. Therefore it would not seem sensible to meta-analyse trials including participants with different learner characteristics.

Assuming two or more trials have been identified, therefore, and have used similar interventions in similar contexts, what is the process? Most educational meta-analyses will involve calculating a pooled effect size. There are a number of different statistical approaches to meta-analysis, which are described in more detail within statistical texts specifically devoted to aspects of meta-analysis (e.g. Lipsey and Wilson 2001). In this chapter only an overview of the main approach is described.

As described previously, an effect size is the difference in means between the two groups divided by either the pooled standard deviation or the standard deviation of the control group, to give a common metric that can be applied to studies using different forms of post-test. The standard deviation is a measure of dispersion for a continuous variable like a test score. A large value for the standard deviation indicates that there is a large spread of values around the mean value. The method for deriving the standard deviation is available from all basic statistical textbooks, and is routinely calculated for statistical output from software packages.

The advantage of calculating a standardized effect size is that it enables comparisons to be made between studies that use very different measures of outcome. For example, two spelling trials were undertaken by MacArthur *et al.* (1990) and McClurg and Kasakow (1989). The study by MacArthur *et al.* used a spelling test out of 20 for the outcome measure, whilst the McClurg and Kasakow trial used a spelling test out of 36. The difference between the groups in the McClurg and Kasakow study was an average of six spellings compared with only two spellings in the McArthur *et al.* trial. However, these differences are not directly comparable as the spelling tests were quite different. By calculating a standardized effect size Torgerson and Elbourne (2002) could show that the MacArthur trial had an effect size of 0.35, whilst the McClurg and Kasakow study had an effect size of 1.15.

Once the effect sizes of each study, with their associated 95% confidence intervals, have been calculated, the next step is to pool all the data in a meta-analysis. We cannot, however, simply average the standardized effect sizes and generate an average as this gives equal weight to all the trials, when in fact the trials with the bigger sample sizes should be given most weight as their results are closer to the 'true' value. Therefore, in the meta-analysis the effect sizes from each trial is 'weighted' by the trial's size. Larger trials receive a greater weight to reflect their greater importance.

Usually the software program that produces the meta-analysis will also produce a graphical display of the effect size of each individual randomized trial with 95% confidence intervals. This is known as a 'forest plot'. A forest plot is a helpful graphical aid when examining all the effect sizes of the identified trials. It can be used to describe all the identified studies even when there is no intention to pool or meta-analyse them.

In Figure 7.1 a typical forest plot shows a meta-analysis of four trials evaluating the effects of using unpaid classroom assistants (volunteers) to help children learn to read. The effect size of each trial is calculated with the appropriate

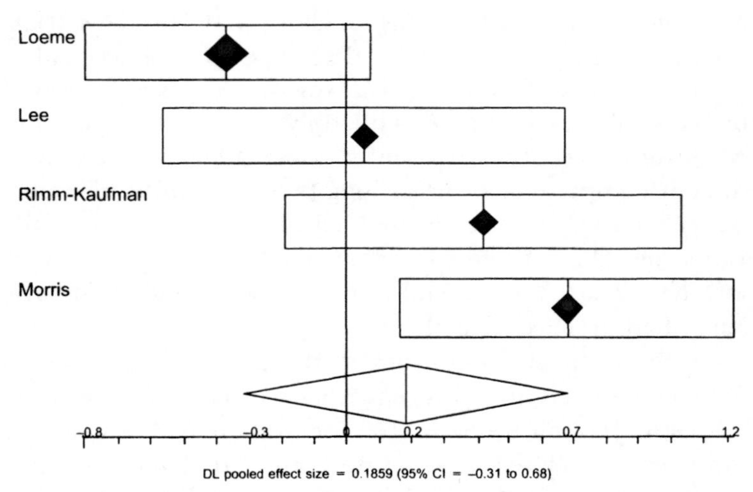

Figure 7.1 Forest plot of randomized trials of the effect of unpaid volunteers on literacy outcomes

95% confidence intervals. Small trials have very wide confidence intervals. This particular meta-analysis is suggestive of an overall benefit of about a fifth of an effect size. The 'pooled' confidence interval, however, is wide (reflecting the small trials that were included), and the overall effect size is not statistically significant. In this instance the use of volunteer assistants is suggestive of benefit but is not conclusive. Indeed, because the confidence interval passes through zero, the use of volunteers could actually worsen educational outcomes. Therefore, this meta-analysis is a powerful pointer towards the need for a large well-conducted trial of volunteer helpers in schools.

If trials use cluster or group randomization (that is the class or school is the unit of randomization) then these cannot be included in a meta-analysis with individually randomized trials.

Meaning of effect sizes

An effect size is a statistical device that facilitates a comparison of the effectiveness of different studies that use disparate measures of effect. It is important, however, to consider what an effect size means in educational practice. In Table 7.3 different effect sizes are translated into proportions passing a test.

If we apply some of these effect sizes at a population level we can see how important even quite small effect sizes can be. If for example, class sizes were reduced from 25 pupils to 15 this would result in an effect size of about 0.15. Applying this to a national school population of say 700,000 taking a particular public exam, this would imply that about 40,000 more children would cross the 50 per cent threshold if smaller class sizes were implemented. Small effect sizes can be worthwhile; however, to detect these modest but important differences requires either a very large trial, like

Table 7.3 Translating effect sizes into pass rates

Mean effect size	Percentage of extra students passing a 50% test threshold
0	0
0.1	4
0.2	8
0.3	12
0.4	16
0.5	19
0.6	23
0.7	26
0.8	29
0.9	32
1.0	34

the Tennessee trial of class sizes, or a systematic review combined with a meta-analysis.

Sensitivity analysis

Sensitivity analyses can be undertaken to test the robustness of the review results. One way of testing the results is to undertake separate analyses on subgroups of trials. For example, do trials that use blinding or masking of post-tests generate similar effect sizes to trials that do not state that blinding was used? Are the results from large trials different from the results from small trials?

Summary

- Data from randomized trials can be synthesized in a number of different ways: 'qualitative' overviews, 'vote-counting' methods, meta-analyses, all of which have their strengths and limitations.

- Meta-analysis allows the detection of small and possibly educationally important effect sizes.
- Whether or not small effect sizes are 'worthwhile' depends upon the nature of the intervention and its cost.

8

Conclusions

Systematic reviews of randomized controlled trials are very important policy tools. If reviews show little evidence of an effect this is an extremely important result. Large amounts of resources are often directed toward interventions where there is little or no evidence of effectiveness. For example, non-randomized data from both the UK and Israel indicate that the large investment in ICT in education may be counter-productive. Israeli data suggest ICT is actually harmful in the learning of mathematics and has no effect in the learning of Hebrew. Systematic reviews of randomized trials of ICT and literacy from the English-speaking world show little evidence of benefit of ICT on the acquisition of literacy, supporting the worrying findings from the non-randomized data (Torgerson and Zhu 2003).

Negative reviews also sound cautionary notes about the need to base policy-making on robust trial data. Whilst undertaking a large rigorous trial of the effectiveness of ICT on literacy would be a relatively expensive piece of research, the cost pales into insignificance compared with the cost of not doing the research.

Similarly, a systematic review of programmes for adult literacy and numeracy uncovered little evidence for any single effective method of improving literacy and numeracy skills among adults (Torgerson, Porthouse, Brooks 2003). Again such a finding is extremely important in terms of the needs for research.

On a positive note, systematic reviews have been

instrumental in showing smaller class sizes are related to improved performance in educational outcomes. Also systematic reviews have shown that phonological awareness training and phonics teaching are effective for improving literacy acquisition among young children (Ehri, Nunes, Stahl, Willows 2001, Ehri, Nunes, Willows *et al.* 2001).

For primary researchers meta-analyses and systematic reviews are important. Ideally, a positive finding of an intervention that is observed in a meta-analysis ought to be confirmed by an appropriately designed trial. Whilst a 'follow-up' trial *can* confirm the findings of a meta-analysis (Hedges 2000), this is not always the case (Fukkink 2002).

Although systematic reviews ought to be an important tool for the policy-maker, even very persuasive findings are not always implemented. The UK government insists on implementing driver education despite strong evidence showing its lack of effectiveness. Nevertheless, one of the aims of research is to reduce uncertainty, and whilst some policy-makers may wish to operate in an evidence-free environment this will not always be the case.

This book has described the first steps that will enable a student or researcher to undertake a systematic review. An important aspect of systematic reviewing, which perhaps has not been emphasized sufficiently, is its collaborative nature. Whilst a systematic review can be undertaken by a single reviewer, and described as such, the quality of the review process is undoubtedly improved by collaboration with various specialists, including information and content specialists, trial methodologists and statisticians.

Systematic reviews will inevitably be 'good, bad and indifferent'. What sets a systematic review apart from the other research tool – the narrative review – is that a systematic review can be re-examined because its methods are explicit and replicable. Controversial findings from a systematic review can be tested using either the same criteria as described by the authors to check for errors or, alternatively, different criteria can be used to include, exclude or combine studies. Often valid criticisms of systematic reviews can be made because they *are* so explicit. This is in contrast to non-systematic reviews, where the methods can often be opaque.

Systematic review techniques were pioneered by educational researchers, but have, to an extent, fallen out of fashion. There is a welcome increased interest in the technique by newer generations of educational researchers.

Suggested Further Reading

Chalmers, I. (2001) 'Comparing like with like: some historical milestones in the evolution of methods to create unbiased comparison groups in therapeutic experiments', *International Journal of Epidemiology*, 30, 1156–64.

Chalmers, I., Hedges, L. V. and Cooper, H. (2002) 'A brief history of research synthesis', *Evaluation and the Health Professions*, 25, 12–37.

Cook, T. D. (2002) 'Reappraising the arguments against randomized experiments in education: an analysis of the culture of evaluation in American schools of education.' Paper for presentation at the SRI International Design Conference on Design Issues in Evaluating Educational Technologies (www.sri.com/policy/designkt/found.html).

Oakley, A. (2000) *Experiments in Knowing: Gender and Method in the Social Sciences*. Cambridge: Polity Press.

Slavin, R. E. (1986) 'Best-evidence synthesis: an alternative to meta-analytic and traditional reviews', *Educational Researcher*, 15, 5–11.

References

Altman, D. G. (1996) 'Better reporting of randomised controlled trials: The CONSORT statement', *British Medical Journal*, 313, 570–1.

Badger, D., Nursten, J., Williams, P. and Woodward, M. (2000) 'Should all literature reviews be systematic?', *Evaluation and Research in Education*, 14, 220–30.

Batchelder, J. S. and Rachal, J. R. (2000) 'Effects of a computer-assisted instruction programme in a prison setting: an experimental study', *Journal of Correctional Education*, 51, 324–32.

Berlin, J. A. (1997) 'Does blinding of readers affect the results of meta-analyses?', *Lancet*, 350, 185–6.

Boruch, R. F. (1994), 'The future of controlled randomised experiments: a briefing', *Evaluation Practice*, 15, 265–74.

Boruch, R. F. (1997) 'Randomized experiments for planning and evaluation: a practical approach', in *Applied Social Research Methods Series 44*. London: Age Publications.

Chalmers, I. (2001) 'Comparing like with like: some historical milestones in the evolution of methods to create unbiased comparison groups in therapeutic experiments', *International Journal of Epidemiology*, 30, 1156–64.

Chalmers, I. and Altman, D. G. (eds) (1995) *Systematic Reviews*. London: BMJ Publishing Group.

Chalmers, I., Hedges, L. V. and Cooper, H. (2002), 'A brief history of research synthesis', *Evaluation and the Health Professions*, 25, 12–37.

Clayton, A. B., Lee, C., Sudlow, D. E., Butler, G. and Lee, T. (1998) *Evaluation of the DSA school's initiatives*. British Institute of Traffic Education Research.

Cochrane Injuries Group Albumin Reviewers (1998) 'Human albumin administration in critically ill patients: systematic review of randomised controlled trials', *British Medical Journal*, 317, 235–40.

Cochrane Injuries Group Driver Education Review (2001) 'Evidence based road safety: the Driving Standards Agency's school programme', *Lancet*, 358, 230–2.

Constable, H. and Coe, R. (2000) 'Evidence and indicators: dialogue, improvement and researching for others', *Evaluation and Research in Education*, 14, 115–23.

Cook, T. D. (2002) 'Reappraising the arguments against randomized experiments in education: an analysis of the culture of evaluation in American schools of education.' Paper for presentation at the SRI International Design Conference on Design Issues in Evaluating Educational Technologies (www.sri.com/policy/designkt/found.html).

Cook, T. D. and Campbell, T. D. (1979) *Quasi-Experimentation: Design and Analysis Issues for Field Settings*. Boston: Houghton Mifflin.

Crain, R. L. and York, R. L. (1976) 'Evaluating a successful program: experimental method and academic bias', *School Review*, 84, 233–54.

Davies, H., Nutley, S. and Smith, P. (2000), 'Introducing evidence-based policy and practice in public services', in H. Davies, S. Nutley and P. Smith (eds), *What Works? Evidence-based Policy and Practice in Public Services*. Bristol: The Policy Press, 1–11.

Davies, H., Nutley, S. and Tilley, N. (2000), 'Debates on the role of experimentation', in H. Davies, S. Nutley and P. Smith (eds), *What Works? Evidence-based Policy and Practice in Public Services*. Bristol: The Policy Press, 251–76.

Davies, H., Laycock, G., Nutley, S., Sebba, J. and Sheldon, T. (2000) 'A strategic approach to research and development', in H. Davies, S. Nutley and P. Smith (eds), *What Works? Evidence-based Policy and Practice in Public Services*. Bristol: The Policy Press, 229–50.

Davies, P. (1999) 'What is evidence-based education?', *British Journal of Educational Studies*, 47, 108–21.

Davies, P. (2000) 'The relevance of systematic reviews to educational policy and practice', *Oxford Review of Education*, 26, 365–78.

DfEE (1989) *The National Literacy Strategy. Framework for Teaching*: London: DfEE.

Egger, M. and Davey-Smith, G. (2001) 'Principles of and procedures for systematic reviews', in M. Egger, G. Smith and D. Altman (eds), *Systematic Reviews in Health Care Meta-Analysis in Context* (2nd edn). London: BMJ Books.

Egger, M., Davey-Smith, G. and O'Rourke, K. (1995) 'Rationale, potentials and promise of systematic reviews', in I. Chalmers and D. Altman (eds), *Systematic Reviews*. London: BMJ Publications Group.

Egger, M., Smith, G. D. and Altman, D. G. (eds) (2001) *Systematic Reviews in Health Care Meta-Analysis in Context* (2nd edn). London: BMJ Books.

Ehri, L. C., Nunes, S. R., Stahl, S. A. and Willows, D. M. (2001) 'Systematic phonics instruction helps students learn to read: evidence from the national reading panel's meta-analysis', *Review of Educational Research*, 71, 393–447.

Ehri, L. C., Nunes, S. R., Willows, D. M., Valeska Schuster, B., Yaghoub-Zadeh, Z. and Shanahan, T. (2001) 'Phonemic awareness instruction helps children learn to read: evidence from the National Reading Panel's meta-analysis', *Reading Research Quarterly*, 36 (3), 250–87.

Evans, J. and Benefield, P. (2001) 'Systematic reviews of educational research: does the medical model fit?', *British Educational Research Journal*, 27 (5), 528–41.

Eysenck, H. J. (1995) 'Problems with meta-analysis', in I. Chalmers and D. Altman (eds), *Systematic Reviews*. London: BMJ Publication Group.

Fitz-Gibbon, C. (2000) 'Education: realising the potential', in H. Davies, S. Nutley and P. Smith (eds), *What Works? Evidence-based Policy and Practice in Public Services*. Bristol: The Policy Press, pp. 69–91.

Fukkink, R. G. (2002) 'Effects of instruction on deriving word meaning from context and incidental word learning', *Educational Studies in Language and Literature*, 2, 38–57.

Fulk, B. M. and Stormont-Spurgin, M. (1995) 'Spelling interventions for students with disabilities: a review', *The Journal of Special Education*, 28 (4), 488–513.

Glass, G. V., (1976) 'Primary, secondary and meta-analysis', *Educational Researcher*, 5, 3–8.

Gough, D. and Elbourne, D. (2002) 'Systematic research synthesis to inform policy, practice and democratic debate', *Social Policy in Society*, 1 (3), 225–36.

Hammersley, M. (1997) 'Educational research and a response to David Hargreaves', *British Educational Research Journal*, 23 (2), 141–61.

Hammersley, M. (2001) 'On "systematic" reviews of research literatures: a "narrative" response to Evans and Benefield', *British Educational Research Journal*, 27 (5) 543–53.

Hargreaves, D. H. (1996) 'Teaching as a Research-based Profession: Possibilities and Prospects.' Teacher Training Agency Annual Lecture. London: Teacher Training Agency.

Hargreaves, D. H. (1997) 'In defence of research for evidence-based teaching: a rejoinder to Martyn Hammersley', *British Educational Research Journal*, 23 (4), 405–19.

Hatcher, P., Hulme, C. and Ellis, A. (1994) 'Ameliorating early reading failure by integrating the teaching of reading and phonological skills: the phonological linkage hypothesis', *Child Development*, 65, 41–57.

Hedges, L. V. (2000) 'Using converging evidence in policy formation: the case of class size research', *Evaluation and Research in Education*, 14, 193–205.

Juni, P., Altman, D. G. and Egger, M. (2001) 'Assessing the quality of randomised controlled trials', in M. Egger, G. Davey-Smith and D Altman (eds), *Systematic Reviews in Health Care: Meta-analysis in Context* (2nd edn). London: BMJ Publishing Group.

Juni, P., Witschi, A., Bloch, R. and Egger, M. (1999) 'The hazards of scoring the quality of clinical trials for meta-analysis', *JAMA*, 282, 1054–60.

Kjaergard, L. L., Villumsen, J. and Cluud, C. (2001) 'Reported methodologic quality and discrepancies between large and small randomized trials in meta-analyses', *Annals of Internal Medicine*, 135, 982–9.

Kulik, J. and Kulik, C. C. (1989) 'Meta-analysis in education', *International Journal of Educational Research*, 13 (3), 220.

Lipsey, M. W. and Wilson, D. B. (1993) 'The efficacy of psychological, educational and behavioural treatment: confirmation from meta-analysis', *American Psychologist*, 48, 1181–209.

Lipsey, M. W. and Wilson, D. B. (2001) *Practical Meta-Analysis*. Applied Social Research Methods Series 49. London: Sage Publications.

MacArthur, C. A., Ferretti, R. P., Okolo, C. M. and Cavalier, A. R. (2001) 'Technology applications for students with literacy problems: a critical review', *The Elementary School Journal*, 101 (3), 273–301.

MacArthur, C. A., Haynes, J. A., Malouf, D. B., Harris, K. and Owings, M. (1990) 'Computer assisted instruction with learning disabled students: achievement, engagement and other factors that influence achievement', *Journal of Educational Computing Research*, 6, 311–28.

Martinson, K. and Friedlander, D. (1994) *GAIN: Basic Education in a Welfare-to-Work Program. California's Greater Avenues for Independence Program*. New York: Manpower Demonstration Research Corporation.

McClurg, P. A. and Kasakow, N. (1989) 'Wordprocessors, spelling checkers, and drill and practice programs: effective tools for spelling instruction?', *Journal of Educational Computing Research,* 5, 187–98.

Mulrow, C. (1994) 'Rationale for systematic reviews', *British Medical Journal*, 309, 597–9.

NHS Centre for Reviews and Dissemination (2001) *Undertaking systematic reviews of research on effectiveness: CRD's guidance for those carrying out or commissioning reviews* (CRD Report No. 4: 2nd edn). York: University of York, NHS Centre for Reviews and Dissemination.

Oakley, A. (1998) 'Experimentation and social interventions: a forgotten but important history', *British Medical Journal*, 317, 1239–42.

Oakley, A. (2000) *Experiments in Knowing: Gender and Method in the Social Sciences*. Cambridge: Polity Press.

Oakley, A. (2002) 'Social science and evidence-based everything: the case of education', *Educational Review*, 54, 277–86.

Petrosino, A., Boruch, R. F., Rouding, C., McDonald, S. and Chalmers, I. (2000) 'The Campbell Collaboration Social Science, Psychological, Educational and Criminological Trials Register (C2-SPECTR) to facilitate the preparation and maintenance of systematic reviews of social and educational interventions', *Evaluation and Research in Education*, 14, 206–19.

Petrosino, A., Turpin-Petrosino, C. and Buehler, J. (2002) ' "Scared straight" and other juvenile awareness programmes for preventing juvenile delinquency.' Campbell Collaboration website www.campbellcollaboration.org/doc-pdf/ssr.pdf

Petticrew, M. (2001) 'Systematic reviews from astronomy to zoology: myths and misconceptions', *British Medical Journal*, 322, 98–101.

Pirrie, A. (2001) 'Evidence-based practice in education: the best medicine?', *British Journal of Educational Studies*, 49, 124–36.

Pring, R. (2000) 'Editorial: Educational research', *British Journal of Educational Studies*, 48, 1–10.

Roberts, I. (2000) 'Randomised trials or the test of time? The story of human albumin administration', *Evaluation and Research in Education*, 14, 231–6.

Schulz, K. F., Chalmers I., Hayes, R. and Altman, D. G. (1995) 'Empirical evidence of bias: dimensions of methodological quality associated with estimates of treatment effects in controlled trials', *JAMA*, 273, 408–12.

Shea, B., Dube, C. and Moher, D. (2001) 'Assessing the quality of reports of systematic reviews: the QUOROM statement compared to other tools', in M. Egger, G. Davey-Smith and D. G. Altman (eds), *Systematic Reviews in Health Care: Meta-analysis in Context* (2nd edn). London: BMJ Publishing Group.

Slavin, R. E. (1986) 'Best-Evidence synthesis: an alternative to meta-analytic and traditional reviews', *Educational Researcher*, 15, 5–11.

Sterne, J. A., Egger, M. and Davey-Smith, G. (2001) 'Investigating and dealing with publication and other biases', in M. Egger, G. Davey-Smith and D. G. Altman (eds), *Systematic Reviews in Health Care: Meta-analysis in Context* (2nd edn). London: BMJ Publishing Group.

Tooley, J. and Darby, D. (1998) *Education Research: An Ofsted Critique*. London: OFSTED.

Torgerson, C. J. and Elbourne, D. (2002) 'A systematic review and meta-analysis of the effectiveness of information and communication technology (ICT) on the teaching of spelling', *Journal of Research in Reading*, 35 (2), 129–43.

Torgerson, C. J. and Torgerson, D. J. (2001) 'The need for randomised controlled trials in educational research', *British Journal of Educational Studies*, 49, 316–28.

Torgerson, C. J. and Zhu, D. (2003) 'A systematic review and meta-analysis of the effectiveness of ICT on literacy learning in English, 5–16' *(EPPI-Centre Review, version 1)*, in *Research Evidence in Education Library*. London: EPPI-Centre, Social Science Research Unit, Institute of Education.

Torgerson, C. J., King, S. E. and Sowden, A. J. (2002) 'Do volunteers in schools help children to learn to read? A systematic review of randomised controlled trials', *Educational Studies* , 28, 433–44.

Torgerson, C. J., Porthouse, J. and Brooks, G. (2003), 'A systematic review and meta-analysis of randomised controlled trials evaluating interventions in adult literacy and numeracy', *Journal of Research in Reading*, 26 (3).

Torgerson, C. J., Brooks, G., Porthouse, J., Burton, M., Robinson, A., Wright, K. and Watt, I. (2003) *Adult literacy and numeracy interventions: Expert, scoping and systematic reviews of the trial literature.* A report to the National Research and Development Centre.

Torgerson, D. J. and Torgerson, C. J. (2003a) 'The design and conduct of randomised controlled trials in education: lessons from health care', *Oxford Review of Education*, 29, 67–80.

Torgerson, D. J. and Torgerson, C. J. (2003b) 'Avoiding bias in randomised controlled trials in educational research', *British Journal of Educational Studies*, 51 (1), 36–45.

Troia, G. A. (1999) 'Phonological awareness intervention research: a critical review of the experimental methodology', *Reading Research Quarterly*, 34, 28–52.

Ukoumunne, O. C., Gulliford, M. C., Chinn, S., Sterne, J. A. C. and Burney, P. G. J. (1998), 'Evaluation of healthcare interventions at area and organization level', in N. Black, J. Brazier, R. Fitzpatrick and B. Reeves, *Health Services Research Methods. London:* BMJ Publications.

Weiner, S. (1994) 'Effects of phonemic awareness training on low- and middle-achieving first graders' phonemic awareness and reading ability', *Journal of Reading Behavior*, 26(3), 277–300.

Wilkes, M. M. and Navickis, R. J. (2001) 'Patient survival after human albumin administration. A meta-analysis of randomized, controlled trials', *Annals of Internal Medicine*, 135, 149–64.

Young, K., Ashby, D., Boaz, A. and Grayson, L. (2002) 'Social science and the evidence-based policy movement', *Social Policy and Society*, 1, 215–24.

Index

CPSIA information can be obtained at www.ICGtesting.com
Printed in the USA
LVOW132151290812

296613LV00010B/61/P